EUCHARIST AND THE LIVING EARTH

Hugh O'Donnell

Eucharist and the Living Earth

the columba press

First published in 2007 by
the columba press
55A Spruce Avenue, Stillorgan Industrial Park,
Blackrock, Co Dublin

Cover by Bill Bolger
Origination by The Columba Press
Watercolours by Michael Moran
Printed in Ireland by ColourBooks Ltd, Dublin

ISBN 978 1 85607 573 2

Table of Contents

Abbreviations

EE, John Paul II, *Ecclesia de Eucharistia*, Encyclical Letter on the Eucharist and the Church, London, Catholic Truth Society, Publishers to the Holy See, 2003

MND, John Paul II, *Mane Nobiscum Domine*, (Abide with us Lord), Apostolic Letter Inaugurating the Year of the Eucharist 2004 -2005, London, Catholic Truth Society, 2004

Acknowledgements

My thanks to my dear mother and (late) father, to brothers and sisters, to my extended family, my adopted Salesian family and to great friends. Thanks also, to the many beings – earthworm, elder, puffball, bluebell, dragonfly, giraffe – whose 'real' presence speaks of the One who 'fathers-forth' in myriad ways through them. More immediately my thanks to Sean McDonagh SSC for his vision in establishing a course in Ecology and Religion with the University of Wales out of which this book grew. To Michael Moran for his delicate watercolour and to the many authors whose wonderful insights enliven the text I am particularly grateful. Finally, a special word of deep appreciation to John Feehan, friend and inspiration, in whose company I first set foot in the wilderness of Slieve Bloom and to whom *Eucharist and the Living Earth* is dedicated.

Father, you are holy indeed,
And all creation rightly gives you praise
(Eucharistic Prayer III)

The role of each and every species is not merely ecological, it
is spiritual;
it is a unique shout of joy, affirmation, worship that no other
species can give.
John Feehan, *The Dipper's Acclaim*[1]

Be praised, my Lord, through all your creatures,
especially through my lord Brother Sun,
who brings the day; and you give light through him.
And he is beautiful and radiant in all his splendour!
Of you, Most High, he bears the likeness.
Francis of Assissi, *Canticle of Brother Sun*

Are we not interested in the cosmos anymore? Are we today
really hopelessly huddled in our own little circle? Is it not important, precisely today, to pray with the whole of creation?
Cardinal Ratzinger, *The Spirit of the Liturgy* (1999)[2]

Foreword

We trace the origin of our Eucharist to the last supper Jesus hosted for his apostles that awful night before the weekend of his passion and death on the cross, events which it enfolds and re-enacts. But we acknowledge that although this is the liturgy of a New Testament its roots are deeper, embedded in the history of the Jewish people and their convenant with the God their history had encountered, and the ritual that surrounded its sacrificial liturgy.

Over this last century and a half, the progress of scientific investigation – which at its core is nothing other than the application of the God-given reason with which we are endowed– has given us an ever-greater understanding of what we are and how we have come to be here. We know that our human beginnings lie somewhere in the savannahs of East Africa rather than in a metaphorical garden in Mesopotamia; and that the dawn of human consciousness was not something altogether new in the world, but the unfolding of a new possibility implicit in all creation from the beginning. The sense of awe that accompanied that awakening of reflective consciousness is of the very essence of human being in the world, and called for a new sort of responsive acclaim: but that dawn of human awareness was not the beginning of worship. As people of faith we believe all that lives proclaims the glory of God: 'All creation rightly gives you praise.' But this is not some general aphorism, as perhaps the psalmist thought or intended: for every voice in life's kaleidoscope, as varied in its fourth dimension of evolutionary time as in this present moment, sounds unique acclaim, 'so that what one lacks in its expression of divine goodness may be compensated for by others: for goodness, which in God is single and undifferentiated, in creatures is refracted into a myriad hues of being'.

There are different levels of acclaim. There is the human acclaim, the robin's acclaim, the acclaim of the rose, all different colours in the kaleidoscope of the acknowledgement and worship of God. Yet – and here is another implication of a deeper understanding of evolution's meaning – this symphony, for all its harmony now and through all time, has its origin in one note, the ultimate OM. It is not just that we have DNA that we share with all that lives: or that this DNA composes in our genomes an ancient, ancient language of which we are learning early and halting words. But more profoundly and ultimate in significance, there is the truth that our human genome is but one haunting, dominant chord in one melody of the symphony of life, to whose One Total Harmony we are utterly attuned, having been born of it and for it, 'the natural inherited wildness in our blood [running] true on its glorious course as invincible and unstoppable as stars' (in the words of John Muir).

Is the acclaim that is asked of us then different in kind? Indeed yes, for we are called to be children of God in a new sense never before seen on earth – for all of life's wondrous and diverse achievement. To us alone it has been given to appreciate God's plan on the level of understanding. But we are fully human only in community. Nothing is more important to individual integrity and self-worth than a sense of belonging, which is why the creation, repair and development of community are a central concern of all modern societies. Every community needs to bring the acclaim of its living into focus through ritual. As humans radiated across the earth from the ancestral home of our species in Africa, there evolved a diversity of ritual form that reflected the adaptive radiation of humankind: a radiation that resulted in the linguistic and cultural diversity that has been the crowning achievement of humanity.

The efflorescence of liturgy is largely a cultural thing: but its roots are deeper and more essentially human. These roots find expression in the simplest of things: gestures, sounds. Human arms held out, palms upturned, mean more than the mere words of any offertory prayer. Where words are to be added, they can only be metaphor. The problem with 'religion' is that the depth and simplicity of that 'primitive' response becomes encrusted with layer after layer of theological elaboration, becoming so deep over time that the heartbeat within is stilled, the awe dulled, the thrill silenced.

The living earth is the very womb within which and out of which we have evolved. Contemplation of its wonder provides our first glimpse of the beauty and goodness of the divine, and is the fount of that concern which has matured over time to include an ethics of responsibility for creation. Over this last century in particular we have seen the diminution of that diversity and of the health of the ecosystems that support it. No contemporary celebration of the Eucharist can fail to take cognisance of this dimming of the rainbow of creation for which we are accountable.

Hugh O'Donnell's book attempts to inform the liturgy of the Eucharist with a new relevance, in the sense not only that it seeks to embrace all we have come to know about our kinship with all creation and our (as yet scarcely-glimpsed) responsibilities in the light of this newly-discovered relationship, but also in the sense that it weaves into the liturgy the notion of our responsibility before God for the well-being and diversity of earth. To some readers what appears in these pages may appear somewhat radical: but so it must be, in the sense in which the gardener prunes the tree back, to the very root sometimes, so that those buds that will flower and set fruit can grow most strongly, not allowing their strength to be sapped by unprofitable growth elsewhere on the tree. Where theology is concerned, the pruning knife should always be kept well-oiled and sharpened: lest we settle in our complacency for a mode of human being that is less than the evolutionary achievement that God's directing hand has breathed into us (and for which the best metaphor perhaps is the human soul) calls us to.

John Feehan
School of Biology and Environmental Science, UCD

Introduction

The need to connect the Eucharist with the Creation story
At a time of rapid cultural change when it could appear that the
Eucharist does not speak meaningfully to us anymore, another
book on the subject must seem superfluous. While it might be
tempting to agree, there is another possibility. It seems that the
Eucharist has become so detached from its matrix within the
created world that it now appears a threadbare ritual with di-
minishing relevance. I would like to explore how this connection can be strengthened; in other words, how the Eucharistic
celebration can be relocated not just within our earthly pilgrimage but within the narrative of an unfolding universe. Viewed in
this way, the Eucharist can recover its dynamic sacramental
reality, and present itself not as a relic of a pre-scientific past,
but as a legitimate and necessary form of worship for Christians
today.

When we fail to make explicit the Eucharistic connection
with the created world, we deny that we are woven into the fabric of the universe; that we live with the stars; that the sun and
the moon leave their mark on our lives. We have forgotten that
Christian liturgy is always a cosmic liturgy. Without this connection we have a ritual shorn of its roots, an impoverished
Eucharist. In *The Spirit of the Liturgy* (1999), Joseph Ratzinger,
now Pope Benedict XVI, opposes the dichotomy which suggests
that nature religions are focussed on the cosmos while the Old
Testament and Christianity are primarily concerned with history.[3]
Rather, he insists, it is only when history and cosmos form 'one
circle of being' that Christian liturgy can shine out in its full
splendour.[4] Addressing the Father in the second Eucharistic
Prayer, we say of Jesus: 'He is the Word through whom you
made the universe, the Saviour you sent to redeem us.' This
makes it clear that redemption and creation are to be seen as two
movements of God's love towards us from the beginning – giv-

ing us life and drawing us close. In this understanding, every breath we take becomes a Spirit-breath for we are 'christened' by virtue of being born.

In the new cosmology that science has revealed to us, 'creation' means more than setting, more than the air we breathe, more than inspiring nature. In this account, we are telling the story of the universe, (not the latest version!) and how we have come to be within that story over 13.7 billion years. To think in terms of an evolutionary journey means that we consider all living beings as essential companions with us on this adventure. This calls for a new way of thinking that will take time, effort and humility. It is worth saying at this point that the new story of creation can be host to a fruitful ecumenical conversation with people of all faiths and of none. Given its truthfulness, it can become our common story, the basis for ongoing religious and ecological reflection. It poses the following question starkly: are we willing to face this moment of environmental crisis together? Our credibility, as people of faith, will be determined by our response. There is no time to lose.

The phrase 'cosmic dimension' occurs throughout this book. It is a phrase that lacks a precise meaning. At one moment it can refer to the natural world, at another to the diversity of created life and our place within it, at another to our living space on a planet circling an ordinary star in a galaxy of billions of stars. A more fruitful understanding, however, is of a cosmic dimension arising from a local, specific setting. In essence, this means that the people of a particular bioregion – the Burren, for example, with its culture, topography and spiritual heritage – will celebrate Eucharist with a different awareness, a reminder that the gospel 'treasure' must be discovered in one's own field. Finding this 'treasure' of our own home place is a real homecoming to origins and to new responsibilities. The cosmic dimension follows, as it were, the flight of the boomerang which forms a wide circle before returning to the hand. That larger arc of our growing awareness of a threatened planet returns us to the 'treasure' of the living world on our own doorstep. G. K. Chesterton catches something of that double-take on the home place in these words:

> How can we contrive to be at once
> Astonished at the world and yet at home in it?
> How can this queer cosmic town …
> Give us at once the fascination of a strange town
> And the comfort and honour of being our own town?[5]

How important it is then to give thanks from where we are, recognising the gift of our local flora, fauna, our culture and history. Sixty years ago, Aldo Leopold called for the development of a land ethic which would enlarge our understanding of community to include soils, waters, plants and animals or collectively: the land. An ethic which would change our role from being conqueror of the land-community to plain member and citizen of it. Even in 1948, at the time of writing *A Sand County Almanac,* he was aware of how his generation had lost their connection with the natural world.

> Your true modern is separated from the land by many middlemen, and by innumerable physical gadgets. He has no vital relation to it; to him it is the space between cities on which crops grow. Turn him loose for a day on the land, and if the spot doesn't happen to be a golf links or a 'scenic' area, he is bored stiff...In short, land is something he has 'outgrown'.[6]

His comments have a contemporary ring to them. It is likely that our separation from nature is more acute and our sense of community now even more narrow. Nevertheless, there is a growing consciousness that seeks to restore these lost connections; in the words of Patrick Kavanagh, 'to grow with nature again as before I grew.'[7] That is why the affirmation of our own place should find its voice within our Eucharistic celebration. When we find reasons to give thanks, we also find reasons to save.

In his encyclical on the Eucharist (2003), Pope John Paul remarks: 'In my numerous Pastoral Visits, I have seen throughout the world the great vitality which the celebration of the Eucharist can have when marked by the forms, styles and sensibilities of different cultures' (*EE* par 51). At this time of environmental crisis, there is an urgent pastoral need for local church leaders to highlight the cosmic dimension of the Eucharist, drawing on the community's rich heritage of music, symbol and text. In a theological sense, no one cultural expression can monopolise the divine; only when taken together in a rich diversity of expression can the human community adequately give praise. This is not simply about 'adaptation' or 'innovation'. What is required, from priest and faithful alike, is that they bring an ecological consciousness to the celebration of the Eucharist, a task primarily of evocation, not addition. It is a question of how to release the wisdom and energy of the Judeo-Christian tradition for the work before us: namely, to save the earth, to enable it to bloom once again. Psalm 64's note of thanksgiving is exemplary in this regard as it describes the mutual relationship between God and creation.

You keep your pledge with wonders,
O God our saviour,
The hope of all the earth
And of far distant isles.

And thus you provide for the earth;
You drench its furrows,
You level it, soften it with showers,
You bless its growth.

You crown the year with your goodness.
Abundance flows in your steps,
In the pastures of the wilderness it flows.

The hills are girded with joy,
The meadows covered with flocks,
The valleys are decked with wheat.
They shout for joy, yes, they sing.

Eucharist in the context of a threatened environment
In adopting Thomas Berry's account of the universe story, I hope to show how the guiding themes of an evolutionary journey, namely, *differentiation, interiority* and *communion*, emerge in a renewed understanding of the Eucharist. His *Dream of the Earth*[8] and *The Great Work*,[9] particularly, outline an unfolding history of creation that is entrancing, a 'story' that we must claim as our sacred story if we are to survive with the other species on this unique planet. He is not the only one to have assimilated the theory of evolution into his theological reflection

but the one to have provided a most enthralling contemporary synthesis. Pierre Teilhard de Chardin did so magnificently in the first half of the twentieth century. Combining in himself, with such refinement, the scientist and the mystic, he shared a liberating vision of how the Eucharist extends and prolongs Christ's presence in creation. The graced insight of *The Mass on the World* and *The Spiritual Power of Matter* sings of the cosmic dimension memorably.[10] Though influenced by Teilhard, Berry cannot share his optimism regarding our common future. At this time of environmental crisis, writes Berry, we must commit ourselves to the survival of the planet. Situating the Eucharist then in the context of a threatened environment enlivens hope in a world degraded through ignorance and greed.

There is a conversion required if we are to allow this new revelation of God's universe to take root in us. In this respect, the call to an 'ecological conversion' enunciated by John Paul II has serious implications for the Christian life.[11] It would seem to call for the development of an 'ecological self,' to use a phrase of Arne Naess. This implies a broadening and deepening of the self away from the gratification of insatiable ego, so as to embrace all life forms.[12] For centuries, we have thought about the earth. An 'ecological self' thinks, feels, loves itself as earth. The self-realisation of a fully human response that he speaks of, includes an identification with all creatures, a development that will challenge our sense of who we are, where we live and how we understand community; how we hear the Word of God; how we celebrate Eucharist.

There is a point that needs to be made about the poor. It is possible to engage in an academic discussion about the threat to individual species and to the earth itself without recalling with Leonardo Boff that the most threatened creatures are not whales but the poor, who are condemned to die before their time.[13] He goes on to explain that the cry of the poor and the cry of the earth are interconnected. Rosemary Radford Ruether expresses it in this way:

> de-forestation means women walk twice as far each day to gather wood. Drought means women walk twice as far each day seeking water. Pollution means a struggle for clean

water largely unavailable to one's people; it means children in shantytowns dying of dehydration from unclean water.[14]

Behind our consideration of a 'cosmic' dimension to the Eucharist is the presence of the poor, that 80% of the human population surviving on less than 20% of the earth's resources. The poorest 20%, over a billion people – mostly women and children – starve and die early from poisoned waters, soil and air. For Eucharistic people who are concerned about 'the fruit of the earth and the work of human hands', her comments apply to us all:

> We must recognize the way in which the devastation of the earth is an integral part of an appropriation of the goods of the earth whereby a wealthy minority can enjoy strawberries in winter, winged to their glittering supermarkets by a global food procurement system, while those who pick and pack the strawberries lack the money for bread and are dying from pesticide poisoning.[15]

The development of an 'ecological self', of a consciousness attuned to the sacred dimension of creation, cannot but deepen our appreciation of Christ's self-offering on behalf of all. In a more integral understanding of our place in the choir, we might profitably adopt these sentiments of Teilhard de Chardin and make his prayer our own.

> Shatter, my God, through the daring of your revelation the childishly timid outlook that can conceive of nothing greater or more vital in the world than the pitiable perfection of our human organism.[16]

It could be objected that referring to a cosmic dimension of the Eucharist is a distraction as Jesus did not have this understanding of the universe story. Or perhaps that the cosmic dimension forces a new interpretation on the Eucharist. On the contrary, created reality is fundamental to what we mean by sacrament. In a deepened understanding, the Eucharist becomes the sacrament of unity of the whole of creation, from the alpha of the first Flaring Forth to the omega of its fulfilment.

CHAPTER ONE

A Cosmic Context

'Its Radiant Mystery' will shine forth in a cosmic celebration
At the time of writing, following the Year of the Eucharist (2004-5), it seems timely that the great Christian mystery, 'the summit and source of the life and mission of the Church,' be set in its widest context (*Ecclesia de Eucharistia, EE*, par 1, 2003). In a crucial sense, the Eucharist can never be the preserve of a particular faith community. As the 'breaking of bread' has always been at the centre of the church's life, Christian communities of varying hues will celebrate and understand Christ's words to 'take and eat, this is my body' with varying inflections of belief and expression. There is a strange religious irony in the tangled history of division surrounding this core sacrament of Christian faith and communion and it is easy to get lost in the detail. My concern is to show how the celebration of Eucharist is enhanced by situating it explicitly (it is there implicitly by the very nature of sacrament) within the unfolding creation.

Despite the vagaries of our evolutionary journey, with its random genetic mutation and natural selection over a vast time-scale, the universe has never been left unattended. This roller-coaster ride, characterised by chance, the struggle to survive, apparent waste, dead ends, tragic outcomes and good luck reminds us that we are part of a truly cosmic journey. It seems that we are meant to be here. The accompanying presence of the Eucharistic Christ within this process is not a divine after-thought. It is there from the beginning as an outpouring of Trinitarian love.

Recent church documents to mark the Eucharistic Year do not dwell on the 'cosmic' dimension which connects Eucharist with the creation story (*EE*, par 8). Their concern is with discipline and renewal so that 'the Eucharist will continue to shine forth in all its radiant mystery' (*EE*, par 10). Nevertheless, in his

Apostolic Letter, *Mane Nobiscum Domine*, (*MND*) (2004), Pope John Paul II is anxious that no dimension of the Eucharist should be neglected: 'It is we who must open ourselves up to the dimensions of the Mystery,' – (including its cosmic dimension) – instead of reducing the Eucharist to our own concerns (par 14). After all, the church draws her life from the Eucharist, is born in 'the breaking of bread' and re-born every time the Eucharist is celebrated. It is this sense of immediacy, of being able to embrace all of (cosmic) history that elicits a 'profound amazement' from the believer (*EE*, par 5).

I believe that 'its radiant mystery' will shine forth not simply when the rubrics are fully observed but when the Eucharist is understood in its widest significance, namely, as expressing Christ's intention to offer his nourishing presence to the whole of creation, from the fireball event of beginnings to this present, threatened moment of existence. When considering the apostolic tradition of facing east in prayer and liturgy, the former Cardinal Ratzinger makes this profound reflection:

> The cosmos is praying with us. It, too, is waiting for redemption. It is precisely this cosmic dimension that is essential to Christian liturgy. It is never performed solely in the self-made world of man. It is always a cosmic liturgy. The theme of creation is embedded in Christian prayer. It loses its grandeur when it forgets this connection.[1]

This extends Christ's longing – 'may they all be one' (Jn 17:21) – to all living beings, and highlights his invitation to 'take and eat' as his way of being intimately present within the universe.

Prior to how we celebrate the Eucharist is the related question, what is liturgy? In simple terms, the point of the drama of liturgy is to stage the play, to breathe life into text, to release its symbolic force by acting it out. The word *play* in this context has nothing to do with being playful or light-hearted. At a deep level it is play which educates our imagination and directs us towards a truth of our existence, namely that, in the celebration of the Eucharist, for example, the common heartbeat of creation is overheard. It is the play of the Spirit over and within the fruits of the earth that brings them to life (the same Spirit 'moving over the face of the waters' in Genesis chapter 1). This play acts out the love story of God and creation contained in the words, 'Take and eat, this is my body which will be given up for you.' It recalls how this creator-God led his people through the wilderness so that they might learn how to worship and live within an accompanying Presence. The result of our Eucharistic drama is that we emerge enlivened, new-born in hope. And hope is the central protagonist in the play of Christian liturgy. The action centres around forsaken hope nailed to the cross as the immense suffering and injustice of human and non-human reality is redeemed in Christ's 'Today you will be with me in paradise.' In the resurrection of Jesus, the whole creation is uplifted.

In an early poem, Seamus Heaney remembers a common incident of home love, the sacramental moment of 'the scone rising to the tick of two clocks.'[2] In the Eucharist there is always that experience of time suspended, of past and future collapsing in a now. A recent Heaney poem dedicated to his great friend and poet, Czeslaw Milosz, has him recall the experience after receiving Communion of 'time starting up again'.[3] It's as if the liturgy of the Eucharist has been played out among us and in the process we have been changed. We are now witnesses who have seen with our eyes, heard and tasted the living Christ. We emerge as the children to whom the kingdom story of fulfilment belongs, a story in which the whole world is implicated. We are returned to our true selves and to specific, important commitments. As Christians, steeped in resurrection hope, we are called to be true participants in the work of creation, knowing ourselves as marvellously and lovingly made together with every other living creature with whom we break the bread of our shared existence and make communion.

Many voices, one hymn of praise
Dietrich Bonhoeffer makes an important distinction between 'the myth of redemption' (which has meaning only after death) and 'the hope of redemption' (which 'sends a man back to his own life on earth in a wholly new way').[4] The latter includes a commitment to this world and acknowledges our place within the whole creation. It suggests that the 'hope of redemption' is expressed by our participation in, and celebration of, the diversity of life. One thinks of St Francis inviting the chirping cricket

to join him in praising the Creator, mingling his own praises with its songs, or in his ecstatically ringing the church bell to rouse the slumbering people of Assisi to come out and enjoy the radiance of a full moon. He understood with such sensitivity how every creature is an agent of celebration, with its own voice, its own reason to praise. We, too, must become aware that the human species is part of a chorus (albeit a central part), as expressed in this canticle: 'O all you works of the Lord, O bless the Lord/ to him be highest glory and praise forever.' It is a chorus of thanksgiving for the delivery from the fiery furnace of the three young Israelites which exhorts the whole of creation to praise: sun and moon, fire and rain, frost and snow, fountains and springs, plants, birds, cattle, sea creatures, wild beasts (Dan 3:40-59).

Modern biology has endorsed our felt notions of kinship so that we now know that physiologically, in biochemical terms, in their genetic make-up, other creatures are on the same level of organisation as we are. And not only have we been swept along on the same evolutionary adventure as all other species but our origins in stardust are similar. This awareness is not designed to put us down so as to raise up the non-human voices. It is to call us to praise in a deeper way, renewing in ourselves the profound insight of Thomas Aquinas who spoke of the Creator and his wish to share his goodness with – (and that goodness to be made manifest in) – his creatures. Since God's

> goodness could not be adequately represented by one creature alone, he produced many and diverse creatures so that, what was wanting to one in the manifestation of divine goodness, might be supplied by another; for goodness, which in God is single and undifferentiated, in creatures is refracted into a myriad hues of being.[5]

St Bonaventure uses a related image to make a similar point. He describes the divine light shining through the stained glass window of creation expressing itself differently in different creatures.

This universal chorus – for we cannot separate ourselves from the earth systems which sustain us nor from other voices raised in praise – is what is implied by the Eucharist as sacrament of unity. ('Unity' understood in an inclusive rather than a restrictive sense.) As such, the Eucharist points to the interrelationship of all beings in the life, death and resurrection of Jesus. By offering up bread and wine, the human community takes the whole earth (and by extension, the universe) in its hands in a gesture of thanksgiving. In the consecrated bread and wine, the entire creation gasps in anticipation of its fulfilment in the heavenly nuptial feast. This 'gathering into one' of all reality is affirmed as we recall how Jesus tore down the dividing wall of enmity and established peace; how he removed the old distinctions between Jews and Gentiles, slaves and free, men and women; how all creation will be recapitulated in Christ (Eph 1:10). In *The Sacrament of Unity*, Walter Cardinal Kasper puts it like this: 'In the Eucharist, the world has once again become one in the praise of the Creator – and this means that the world has become whole.'[6] He sees the recovery of the universal, cosmic dimension of the Eucharist as a prelude to an encounter with the ancient natural religions of Asia, Africa and Latin America and with nonreligious movements, such as New Age. Consequently, he opposes individualistic cut-down versions of the Eucharist or the modern reduction of the Mass to a narrow community perspective.[7] For him, the Eucharist is always 'the liturgy of the world' which, in Teilhard's idiom, gives the cosmos its direction and urges it on. (As will become clearer, references to the 'earth' cannot stand apart from its atmosphere, its sun and moon and its place in the galaxy we call The Milky Way. Consequently, it is entirely correct to speak in terms of a liturgy of the Milky Way or the Mass of the universe.)

The Dipper's aclaim

In his excellent essay, *The Dipper's Acclaim*, John Feehan offers us a nuanced understanding of how each species is so finely attuned to its ecological niche that it becomes the spirit of its own place. He takes the dipper *cinclus cinclus*, a bird of fast-flowing streams and rivers, as an example of the subjectivity of each creature which allows it to respond out of its own environment to acclaim creation. Elaborating on its closeness to us he writes:

> Its heart beats like ours, but tuned to the sound of the waterfall, its blood flows like ours but modulated to the swirl of

the current. Its brain is ... geared ... for a joy that affirms the goodness in the differentness of its experience of the one corner of creation it knows best, better than any other creature. Its spirit and soul are as ours on this profound level, not in some superficial way, for truly was it created with the same loving care. The role of each and every species is not merely ecological, it is spiritual; it is a unique shout of joy, affirmation, worship that no other species can give.[8]

What is astonishing about these words is the way they re-connect 'animal' and 'spiritual,' 'winged creature' and 'worship'. These combinations do not sit easily with us. We are more likely to think of creatures, when we do, as off-cuts from the Creator's bench, doodles, marginalia to amuse while our self-conscious species was taking shape. But to think of them offering 'worship' is challenging on many levels. Do we worship the same Creator? And how do they relate to Christ, 'the first-born of all creation?' It is salutary to recall how little we know of other species, their habits and habitats, their life-cycles and integrity. Sad, too, to think how easily we can excuse ourselves for such ignorance by claiming to be more concerned about knowing God. Thomas Aquinas would have none of it.

Knowing the nature of things helps destroy errors about God ... They are wrong who say: the idea that one has of creatures is not important for faith, provided one thinks correctly about God. An error about creatures results in a false idea of God.[9]

Equally, an error about the living Earth gives us a false idea about God and about ourselves. We cannot say, 'Our task is to feed the hungry, the Earth can look after itself.' On the contrary. Living beings are part of a larger organism, the Earth, which is alive. Astronauts who have seen the Earth from 'outside' have remarked how stunningly beautiful she is. If we could see God's goodness manifest in her sick body, we would immediately rush to her side. Instead we continue to treat her as an object and do not see the 'irreligious' nature of our activity. Ominously, we fail to see that we are one body; when we destroy the Earth we destroy ourselves and the rest of creation.

It becomes important for us to educate ourselves about bio-

diversity and what threatens it: habitat loss, pollution, the introduction of exotic species, over-harvesting and disease. At present, approximately one and three quarters of a million species
have been described and summarily named out of a probable
figure ranging from 10 to a 100 million. Meanwhile, by the
hour, a mode of divine presence flickers out with the extinction
of yet another species. On many levels, we miss these fellow
creatures, but especially as soul friends in their unique articulation of (divine) life.

Such an insight should alert us to relationships with creatures which we take for granted. We treat them variously as
pets, as exhibits, as food, as merchandise, as trophy, as suitable
for experimentation. Our range of response can move from sentimentality to downright cruelty. The manner of rearing, trans-
portation and slaughter of animals has become an ethical issue
for us. And not simply because animals have rights and invite a
moral response from us – a claim disputed by some as quasi-
legal human discourse – but because they are creatures whom
God has called into being. Even a dead pigeon, I suspect, deserves a moment's reflection:

> stiff in his feathery bed with the black flies massed on the
> window ... entry to an unused house a mistake ... his grow-
> ing distress at failure to fly free, to find the sky again, the
> endless battering against the pane. And yet the Father knows
> of such distress (Mt 6:26). Perhaps this death, too, (along with
> the extinction of whole species) is caught up in the cross and
> resurrection of Jesus, an event in which the natural world
> shuddered and graves coughed up their dead (Mt 27:51-4).

Our traditional estimate of creatures needs this caution. They
are not simply irrational, servile beings who exist solely for the
benefit of humans, but in their own right they exist as an integral
part of creation. The banter in the following poem of mine catches
with some humour the essence of the debate.

Monkfish
Unlike the shellfish and the rainbow trout,
you thought it, 'the most revolting thing,
a mouth to put you off swimming for good.
Could you imagine anyone eating that?'

For the three days we went along you had it
in for him; 'plain ugly, ugly as sin.'
'God's creature, something more than food,'
I ventured. 'Will you listen to him!'

For the Shona people of Zimbabwe there is traditionally no debate. 'In the Mutupo myth,' writes Tumani Mutasa Nyajeka,

> a human clan adopts another species and covenants that 'its people shall be our people.' A common commitment to protect one another's survival is established with the assumption that the non-human will understand … The relationship is understood as the vantage point from which one experiences and comes to know the universe.[10]

This understanding is built on three principles: the oneness of all things (thereby challenging hierarchical arrangements); the inherent freedom with some rights-to-be of everything that exists; God (*Mwari*) as the mysterious source (the large slippery rock which only the healthiest can climb!) who keeps everything in being. The adoption of a totem animal allows them a non-human perspective on the created world and shows them their place within the circle of life. In the spendthrift West, in contrast, we live under the delusion that we can flourish apart from the rest of the living world. Ignorance of our origins that reach back two million years (not just to 8,000 years of recorded history) permits us to think of ourselves as atomised moderns who have outstripped our humble roots. Only a retrieval of our being-with-other-creatures can save us from the worst excesses of living out a virtual existence. As we have lost contact with life's rich diversity and our place within it, we have deepened our loneliness. A profound home-sickness accompanies such a loss of connection. As fellow creatures ourselves, we badly need to recover our common roots and our common destiny. In the following, I try to imagine it from the animal's side.

Best Friends
This bundle of dog racing up and down the beach
wants so badly to sleep within hearing of a human voice.
His great sadness – how deep our failure to simply be
there at the window sometimes, to open up, play. Stay.

St Ciarán went further. According to the annals, he founded a religious community with the local animals at Saighir. The following account of the origins and strict discipline of the 'monk's' way of life is worth reading. It recalls the intimacy achieved between the monks who withdrew from human company – following the example of the hermits in the Egyptian desert – and the animals they encountered in those remote places. Little did the saints realise when they entered the wilderness that the God they sought would encounter them in surprising ways. The history of those encounters carries a compelling truth to our generation. They are not simply moral fables like those of Aesop. They bring us face to face with our own flight from nature and our failure to commune with other creatures. The story goes that

when Saint Kieran arrived at Saighir, the first thing he did was sit under a certain tree, in whose shade a ferocious wild boar was lying. At first when he saw the man, the boar fled in terror, but then he was made gentle by God and became a disciple of Kieran in that place just like any monk. Afterwards other animals came to Saint Kieran: namely a fox, a badger, a wolf and a deer: they remained tame in his presence, and obeyed him in everything, just as though they were monks.

But the day came when the fox, being shiftier and more sly than the other animals, stole the sandals of his abbot, holy Kieran himself, and abandoning his vocation, took them away with him to his former lair in the wilderness, wishing to eat them there in peace. Knowing this, holy father Kieran called another of his monks to bring back his erring brother. The badger, because he was a creature skilled in the ways of the woods, obediently headed off in search of the thief, quickly picked up the trail and arrived at the lair of brother fox. Finding him about to eat his lord's sandals the badger cut off the fox's two ears and his tail, and plucked his fur, and then compelled him to come back with him to his monastery, so that he might atone for his theft. The fox, having little choice in the matter, accompanied the badger, and they arrived back at none with the sandals undamaged. And the holy man said to the fox, 'Brother, why have you done this evil thing which does not become a monk. You know that the water here is sweet and free to us all, and likewise we all eat the same food. And if you had a yearning for flesh, almighty God would have provided it from the trees of the wood for us to give to you. So then the fox, begging forgiveness, did penance for his deed, and from then on he only ate what he was told to eat, living out his days as one of the brothers.[11]

Far-fetched and good-humoured, sentimental, or a story that shelters the same instinct about kinship that fired St Francis centuries later? The old monks were on to something alright.

Our first awakening is as participants in creation. And though 'stewardship' is the preferred ethical response of Christianity to human and non-human relationships, it needs to be grounded in 'participation'. Otherwise it can seem foolish pride to think we could ever be clever enough to regulate the Earth. 'Stewardship' also suggests that God has left things in our careless hands in a curious lapse of self-interest, especially given how easily the steward assumes the role of proprietor. In James Lovelock's provocative words: 'We are no more qualified to be the stewards or developers of the Earth than are goats to be gardeners.'[12] Our sense of ourselves as participants, on the other hand, allows us to appreciate the tragic ambivalence of many of our 'interventions' – whether to clear a nest of wasps or ask sacrifices of other species for our well-being.

To discuss the ethical/spiritual significance of other creatures does not result in a biotic egalitarianism (all beings being equally equal) but draws attention to the subjectivity and interdependence of each living thing. Given our particular gifts of rational evaluation, aesthetic appreciation and moral perception we may claim a central place in God's creation but not an exclusive one. The dipper, too, expresses his 'yes' to his God-given place uniquely. So does each creature from bacteria to whale. The glory of God (to adapt Irenaeus) is the creature fully alive in its acclamation. In psalm 57, we invite the whole of creation to become a song with us for we are insufficient for what we want to express: 'Awake, my soul! Awake, O harp and lyre! I will awake the dawn!' This recalls Aquinas' reflection that the whole universe together participates in the divine goodness more per-

fectly, and represents it better, than any single creature whatso-
ever. Eucharistic praise requires such a symphony.

Indeed, this insight recalls the Easter Preface in which 'the
joy of the resurrection renews the whole world' with the answering 'holy, holy, holy' of the heavenly choirs resounding
through all creation (cf Is 6:1-3). Does Christian hope for creation
then, as expressed in the Eucharist, not impel us to take the multiple threats to its survival seriously? So seriously, that at the
Dismissal we go out to make peace with every living thing with
whom we have offered praise, to embody what we have already
acknowledged in the 'sign of peace', recognising with Eucharistic
eyes a brother, sister, mother. It is in the acknowledgment of this
widest possible context that the fullness of Christ's offering to
the Father can be fully appreciated.

The altar of the world
Clearly, there are many dimensions to the Eucharist and 'no dimension of this sacrament should be neglected' (*MND*, par 14).
In the encyclical *EE*, there is a poetic and memorable description
of the cosmic dimension by the late Holy Father as he recalls, in
language and spirit reminiscent of Teilhard de Chardin, his life
as a priest:

> I have been able to celebrate Holy Mass in chapels built along
> mountain paths, on lakeshores and seacoasts; I have celebrat-
> ed it on altars built in stadiums and in city squares ... This
> varied scenario of celebrations of the Eucharist has given me
> a powerful experience of its universal and, so to speak, cos-
> mic character. Yes, cosmic! Because even when it is celebrat-
> ed on the humble altar of a country church, the Eucharist is
> always in some way celebrated on the altar of the world. It
> unites heaven and earth. It embraces and permeates all cre-
> ation. The Son of God became man in order to restore all cre-
> ation, in one supreme act of praise, to the One who made it
> out of nothing (par 8).

Following on Pope John Paul's reflection, one thinks immediately
of the Mass rocks dotted around Ireland, a memory in stone of
the Penal Times when both priest and people, in a sense, were
on the run, where the Passover had to be eaten hastily 'with a

girdle round your waist, sandals on your feet, a staff in your hand' (Ex 12:11).These are special places still known to us, symbolic of values no longer current. In their quiet way, they remind us that the absence of fine building does not deter the miracle from happening. Indeed, the ideal context might be weather-wild and out-of-doors, a hint that weather inclines to be part of the celebration. In her poem, 'The Emigrant Irish', Eavan Boland critiques the modern attitude of dumping what we consider to be 'old'. She recalls how the beautiful oil lamps of our grandparents' time were thrown out with the arrival of electricity. But the oil lamps, she suggests, were symbolic of the values that enabled the emigrants to survive, namely 'Patience. Fortitude. Long-suffering \ in the bruise-coloured dusk of the New World.\ And all the old songs. And nothing to lose.' It's time we re-visited our holy sites and the lives of our ancestors who 'would have thrived on our necessities'.[13]

Worth recalling in this context is an incident related by Bao Ruowang in his book, *Prisoner of Mao*, describing his years in Chinese labour camps. 'The last extraordinary experience I had at Qinghe was the Christmas Mass of Father Hsia.' The team of eighteen men, of which Bao was the leader, were marking out boundaries for rice paddies in temperatures close to zero with a force five wind roaring down from the northwest. It was about 9.30 when he noticed a solitary figure approaching him across the strip. He could tell from the gait that it was Hsia. The old priest asks if he can have a little time to say Mass as it is Christmas Day and Bao obliges. 'He smiled gratefully and scurried away across the road and down the embankment to a dry gully where a bonfire was burning, and where he was shielded from the wind and the view of the warders.' His concluding remarks on this episode are memorable:

A quarter of an hour later, I saw a bicycle against the sky in the distance – a warder was on his way. I hustled over the gully to warn Hsia. As I looked down the embankment I saw that he was just finishing up the Mass, in front of a mound of frozen earth which he had chosen as an altar. He was making the traditional gestures of priests all over the world. But his vestments here were ragged work clothes; the chalice, a chipped enamel mug; the wine, some improvised grape juice; and the host a bit of *wo'tou* he had saved from break-fast. I watched him for a moment and I knew quite well it was the truest Mass I would ever see. I loped down the em-bankment, and when the warder passed on his bike he saw only two prisoners warming their hands.[14]

What is special about this episode is its location literally on this earth. It is a celebration completely outlawed by the state which in some vague sense seems to sense its power. The celebrant is a prisoner, the poorest of the poor whose concern is to celebrate the feast of Incarnation despite all threats to his safety. And what of the two prisoners warming their hands? In Christian symbolism it reminds us of Peter's betrayal around a fire (Jn 18:17) and then, in a post-resurrection story, Jesus' preparing food on a charcoal fire for his grieving and exhausted disciples. Both accounts are necessary for our understanding and, strangely, both take place out of doors. 'On the night he was betrayed' is part of the sacred meal as much as 'come and have breakfast' (Jn 21:12). And what of the fire? It enters into our imagination as part of the eucharistic memory – this primordial element to which we are intimately related. In the Eucharist we recall, according to Teilhard, how 'the (creative) flame has lit up the whole world from within ... that one might suppose the cosmos to have burst spontaneously into flame.'[15]

The point is, what happens when the roof of our understand-ing is lifted regarding our celebration of the Eucharist? One story from the life of Francis of Assisi has the saint climbing to the roof and tearing off the tiles of a humble house that the friars had built for themselves. It would seem that he was leading his brothers towards a larger picture, alerting them to how easily the Spirit can be trapped in a mentality whose concern is primar-ily one of defence, control and security. In the words of Isaiah: 'With heaven my throne and earth my footstool, what house could you build me, what place could you make for my rest?' (66:1). Perhaps, that is why one must become a 'fool' to the pre-vailing culture, as Francis did, to rebuild the house of God on the basis of simplicity, poverty and the gospel. Francis, as patron saint of ecology, presents himself as *homo alterius saeculi*, a man of a new age. His foolishness is not a romantic silliness but an embodied insight whereby he came to understand all beings as having a common origin in the motherly heart of a loving Father. His gentleness, his conversations with bird, flower and animal, his practical care for every living thing, his way of non-possession may be foolishness in the extreme but for us they constitute an essential wisdom for an ecological age. The saintliness and sanity of this most affectionate man challenge us. Sharing in his commitment will deliver us to a deeper level of being, to mysterious presence, to the sacred heart of matter. Of course, deconstructing our thinking will prove a much greater task than bulldozing a building.

Community of all living beings
Within this reflection is the desire to salvage the richness of the Eucharist from an over-emphasis on rubric and a kind of reverence that etherealises rather than incarnates. In other words, a desire to locate the Eucharist in its natural setting among a people on pilgrimage; but a people on pilgrimage also in an evolutionary sense, together with the whole natural world. As St Paul writes so beautifully:

> From the beginning till now the entire creation, has been groaning in one great act of giving birth; and not only creation, but all of us who possess the first-fruits of the Spirit, we too groan inwardly as we wait for our bodies to be set free (Rom 8:22-3).

To our ears, Paul is talking of the Christian God in an evolutionary context. For the biologist, everything that exists is interconnected and interrelated at all levels, whether it be the cell, the organism, the ecosystem, or the planetary community. Rather than threatening our image of God, this picture of the evolution of life corresponds to the way a communal, relational God might create, namely, a Trinitarian God. Furthermore, an evolutionary perspective suggests that the Eucharist 'stands at the centre' not only of the church community but of the community of all living beings – at the centre of a rain forest, for example, 'seething with perhaps ten million species of organisms, every individual member of every species being itself a community of communities of domesticated bacteria.'[16]

The ecological/biological understanding of community is concerned with the mutual interactions of plant, animal, micro-organism in a particular habitat. It describes how different species bond (symbiosis) – the ingenious ways by which one organism associates with another, sometimes for mutual benefit, in other cases apparently not. The plant-fungus partnership on which so much of life on land depends belongs to the former. The mutual symbiosis of mycorrhizal fungi, (which absorb phosphorus and other chemicals from the soil), and the root systems of plants, (which return the compliment with a supply of carbohydrates), gives more than a metaphorical meaning to the word community. Or quite spectacularly, the relationship that exists between the Large Blue butterfly, *Maculinea arian*, and the red ants, *Myrmica*, who provide a nest and a diet of ant grubs for the over-wintering caterpillar until it pupates. On the other side, parasitism seems to us less attractive. The hunting wasp immobilises the bluebottle, her target prey, by attacking the nervous system. She then lays an egg on its body so that her growing larva will have a ready supply of fresh meat available until fully grown. To our sensitivity, this is a painfully slow death for the fly and we may wonder why it has to be so. William Blake raises a similar question in the poem 'The Tyger':

When the stars threw down their spears,
And water'd heaven with their tears,
Did he smile his work to see?
Did he who made the Lamb make thee?[17]

The poem ends with a question: Is it possible that violence is part of a loving plan? Did the Creator arrange things in this way? Indeed, why, on another level, did the meek Lamb that was Jesus (and the other meek lambs of history) have to suffer so horribly? Questions multiply and cosy images of God are shaken.

We, too, are admirable hosts with our own flora and fauna from head lice, crab lice, human bot flies to human fleas, roundworms, tapeworms, fungi, bacteria. Most of us carry around on our foreheads two kinds of mites: one, *Demodex folliculorum*, dwells in the hair follicles, the other, *Demodex brevis*, in the sebaceous glands. Are these other lives not so intimate to us that we cannot dust them off, so to speak, as if a de-lousing is required before we offer praise at the Eucharist? Are they not somehow part of the Body of Christ? It doesn't seem possible at any level to stand alone as if we can present a cut-out version of ourselves whole and entire. The more we see ourselves as integral with all of life, the less we will take offence at the whole creation sharing with us in the 'first fruits of the Spirit'.

This broader vision of what community could mean is eschewed by an exclusively anthropocentric (human-centred) understanding of salvation. In his Apostolic Letter for the Year of the Eucharist, the late Holy Father writes: 'Jesus Christ stands at the centre not just of the history of the church, but also the history of humanity. In him, all things are drawn together (cf Eph 1:10; Col 1:15-20)' (*MND*, par 6). In the encyclical, *Dominum et Vivificantem* (1986), however, he had written more explicitly of the 'cosmic dimension' of the Incarnation by which Christ unites himself not only with the entire reality of humanity but with the whole creation.[18] Surely Christ's role as Word of the Father extends beyond the confines of our own species, given the relational nature of all life. The proclamation of Christ as 'the goal of human history, the focal point of the desires of history and civilisation, the centre of mankind' (*EE* par 6), needs a deeper resonance. St Anselm's praise of Mary strikes such a cosmic note:

> O woman, full and more than full of grace, all creation has received of the overflow of your fullness and its youth has been renewed ... through your blessing all creation is blessed. Not only is creation blessed by the creator, but creation blesses its creator.[19]

It is worth recalling Jesus' exchange with the Canaanite woman as recorded by Matthew (15:21-8) and Mark (7:24-30). It proves to be an important moment for Jesus to find his avowed mission 'only to the lost sheep of the House of Israel' being questioned by an outsider. Her reply to his demeaning remark about throwing the children's food to the house-dogs is classic repartee, 'But even house-dogs eat the scraps that fall from their master's table.' This memorable encounter is more than sentimental. It arises out of a mother's need to have her daughter healed. It asks: is healing to be restricted to a particular race of people? Is Jesus' feeding only for the Jews? The conclusion of this episode in the daughter's healing suggests that it is not. Regarding the

Eucharist, we might go on to ask similar questions. To whom does it belong? Who may come to the table? Are there conditions? The Eucharist is an action of the whole community which includes the 'acclaim' of the whole of life. From an ecological perspective, we are in need of a similar encounter with a 'Canaanite woman' to question our inherited certainties. Perhaps, this time she will belong to another species or speak as an ecosystem. Are we prepared to listen?

Is there a place for Jesus in the new cosmology?
Behind this question is the hint that the Jesus we have come to know and describe is tied to one worldview. St Paul, particularly, recognised in the risen Jesus the cosmic Christ who is 'before all things and in whom all things hold together' (Col 1:17). In contemporary spirituality there is a tendency, however, to interpret the cosmic Christ apart from the historical figure of Jesus, which serves to undermine his place in the creation story. For Christians, a personal and unbreakable connection exists between Jesus and the glorified Christ for it is in the human face and body of Jesus that we discover God. This is reinforced when Jesus' flesh is made the touchstone of continuing in his company: 'Unless you eat the flesh of the Son of Man and drink his blood, you have no life in you. Those who eat my flesh and drink my blood have eternal life' (Jn 6:53-4).

Paul Collins reflects that most Christians are gnostics who don't wish to take the Incarnation seriously, nor as a result, take the cosmos seriously either. He writes: 'It is crystal clear that the flesh of Jesus is basic to the definition of who Christ is.'[20] As far as Eucharistic celebration is concerned, the cosmic Christ alone is not enough. It is the earthiness of the Incarnation that is the remarkable feature of Christianity for it is in matter that God is revealed. Christ is not just the centre of history but, for Paul Collins, is the ultimate symbol that God takes the world seriously.[21] God takes the poor seriously also which is a further reason, according to Seán Freyne, why we must keep the memory of Jesus alive.

> The Galilean dimension of Jesus' career … has entered Christian theological discourse, not as nostalgic biography but as a statement of God's concern for human marginality and particularity. Our continued preoccupation with the his-

34

torical Jesus is indeed justified if this aspect of the memory of Jesus is kept alive and active in our world, especially since Christian belief in his Lordship can easily de-humanise and de-personalise that memory.[22]

(God's concern extends equally to the 'marginality and particularity' of the non-human and to their hope of fulfilment.)

The tendency to embrace a cosmic Christ without earthly roots then is not Christianity. Eucharistic spirituality requires a memory of a real man at a particular time, doing particular actions. In Eucharistic Prayer IV we recall that Christ offers his life as 'the acceptable sacrifice which brings salvation to the whole world'. Without his 'bodily' presence, how can the Eucharist sponsor an environmental ethic of 'participation'? To speak of the cosmic Christ alone may sound inclusive, but it fails to secure the place of Jesus in the new cosmology. In effect, a 'cosmic' dimension of the Eucharist requires there being one who 'wears man's smudge and shares man's smell,' (Hopkins)[23]

'Take and eat this, all of you, and eat it with the Holy Spirit'
In a recent book on the Creator Spirit, entitled *Breath of Life*, Denis Edwards reminds us that the Spirit of God always accompanies the Word. He feels that in Western Christianity, in its theology and spirituality, there has been a tendency to focus exclusively on the Christ person to the exclusion of the Spirit.[24] Certainly, in our Nicene Creed we speak of the Spirit as the 'giver of life', but to what extent do we include all creatures as gifted with Spirit-life? Certainly, to accept that the Spirit is to be found in every creature (an understanding with a long history) challenges our preconception that God is focused only on the human. In an adequate theology of creation it becomes clear that it is the Spirit's personal presence in all creatures that enables them to emerge, to evolve, and to commune with other species in their ecosystem. This view of the sustaining Spirit gives the lie to the dualistic mentality that would denigrate matter and place God outside creation. On the contrary, it implies that the Spirit suffers as we make war on creation.

Sadly, this kind of understanding is undeveloped in Catholic teaching and, as a result, the natural world, as the place of encounter with the divine, is sold short. It is absent, too, from a Eucharistic spirituality that invokes the Spirit (*epiclesis*) over the bread and wine but downplays the activity of the same Spirit in respect of other forms of life which are not deemed to be on our level. In *Women, Earth, and Creator Spirit,* Elizabeth A. Johnson finds an important linkage with the devalued poles of hierarchical dualism:

> Neglect of the Spirit has a symbolic affinity with the marginalization of women and is an inevitable outcome of a sexist, dualistic lens on reality, which also, let us remember, disvalues nature.[25]

The Spirit, humorously described by her as 'an edifying appendage to the doctrine of God,' by being connected with the female role of giving birth and holding things together, finds itself 'the poor relation in the Trinity ... even the Cinderella of theology'.[26] Splitting off the redemptive action of Jesus from the good news revealed in creation (or Word from Spirit), however unintentionally, means that the Eucharist is compartmentalised and the creation undervalued. There is a striking expression used by St Ephrem to highlight the inseparable connection between Christ and the Holy Spirit which deserves attention:

> He called the bread his living body and he filled it with himself and his Spirit ... He who eats it with faith, eats Fire and Spirit ... Take and eat this, all of you, and eat it with the Holy Spirit ... (*EE*, par 17, italics mine).

Ephrem's concept of a Eucharist that involves eating Fire and Spirit, of being 'filled with the Holy Spirit,' is startling. It implies that the reception of the Eucharistic and Creative Spirit drives us out to communion with all creation and validates the goodness of our earthly life. It is well to remember that we are loved not only as a consequence of Christ's action, but because we are! ('God so loved the world that he gave his only Son' (Jn.3: 16; see also 1 Jn 4: 9-10).

'Why are you persecuting me?' (Acts 9: 4)
As we prepare to celebrate the Eucharist and 'call to mind our sins,' is our neglect of creation not a most appropriate matter for attention, especially in the light of earth offering up bread and

wine to sustain us? Patriarch Bartholomew of Constantinople makes it clear:

> For humans to cause species to become extinct and to destroy the biological diversity of God's creation, for humans to degrade the integrity of the earth or its natural forests, or destroy its wetlands, for humans to contaminate the earth's waters, its land, its air and its life with poisonous substances, these are sins.[27]

Are these activities not, in truth, sins against the Holy Spirit, the Lord and Giver of Life as they cut into the quick of life? There is no just war theory in a war on creation where creatures are denied all 'rights' to habitat and to their place in the biosphere, where the Earth is treated as a nonentity. To talk of moral fault only in terms of personal human relationships at a time when the pressing issues are how we deal with global sins against life itself falls short of a full response. Addressing sins against life – our unqualified acceptance of the dictates of corporate and business interests, neglect of the pollution of the living Earth on our doorstep, our failure to welcome succeeding generations with at least the level of abundance we found here – must call us back to the healing place of reconciliation, to the Lord of creation crucified on a tree. Any attempt to separate ourselves off from the rest of 'the body,' in this wider understanding, makes us, in some sense, 'unworthy' of participating fully in the Eucharist (1 Cor 11:27-31). Sean McDonagh elaborates on this theme: 'today we are more and more aware that this one body (because 'there is one bread'), encompasses the body of all created reality' (1 Cor 10:17).[28]

The foregoing has been attempting to take up the cosmic dimension of the Eucharist and to draw out some implications for a celebration that is neither narrowly focused on ourselves nor afraid of the new and startling knowledge about our origins that science has revealed to us. I recall Cardinal Kasper's insistence that we maintain 'with absolute firmness that the human person is the centre and summit of all reality (GS 12),' but an agreed meaning for 'centre and summit' is not to be presumed.[29] If the universe has blossomed into self-consciousness in us, we cannot claim the credit. Rather, the phrase 'centre and summit' indicates that we have responsibilities not given to other creatures. It emphasises difference, not dominion. For every creature, made with the same loving attention as we are, is the centre of its own 'world,' so consummately attuned to its habitat that it becomes the spirit of its own place. The uniqueness of our human species is not threatened by being placed in its natural setting with the rest of creation which God saw to be 'very good' (Gen 1:31).

Our ancestors understood the dependent relationships we share with animals, recognised the spirit in them and revered them for giving up their lives for us. The caves of Altamira (Spain) and Lascaux (France) testify to that, where the numinous paintings of deer, bison and woolly ponies, of shamans disguised as animals, and hunters with their spears can still stir from the walls in the tremble of candlelight. In a supermarket age where the killing is done off-stage, so to speak, the wisdom of dependency seems further off than ever. It would no doubt be a finer thing to see the human being striving to be a 'centre' in terms of wonder and praise – accepting, protecting, fostering – instead of being central in the mindless destruction of our shared home. As a matter of urgency, the question this generation needs to hear addressed from our living planet is, 'Why are you persecuting me?' (Acts 9:4).

CHAPTER TWO

Telling the New Story

Tell me a story.

In this century, and moment, of mania,
Tell me a story.

Make it a story of great distances, and starlight.

The name of the story will be Time
But you must not pronounce its name.

Tell me a story of deep delight.[1]

We must be grateful to the scientific community for so many discoveries. Two of them are particularly relevant to our growing understanding of our place in the universe. One, the notion of 'geological time' that has moved us away from a six thousand year biblical history to a glimpse of a divinity that is much more than an exalted version of ourselves. Nicolaus Steno (1638-86) first understood that fossils could be used to reconstruct a sequence of events in the history of Earth and of life. The idea of cosmic time, however, dates from one day in 1788 when James Hutton took his friends James Hall and John Playfair to examine the strata of Old Red Sandstone along the Berkshire coast in Scotland. That discovery of geological time also made possible modern geology, biology, physics and astronomy. A further important result was to discover how little we knew. Our ignorance has grown with each new discovery as a kind of blessing, encouraging a sense of humility to realise that our human time on earth is but a milli-fraction of cosmic time.

The other great discovery of the last century belongs to the astronomer Edwin Hubble who realised that the universe is expanding (although Einstein's general theory of relativity ten years earlier had made such a prediction). Of course, in 1917 it was thought that the Milky Way was the entire universe. Using the famous 100-inch Hooker Telescope, which began operating in 1918, Hubble discovered that what looked like fuzzy patches of light in lesser telescopes were actually other galaxies. It became evident that our Galaxy of about 100,000 light years in diameter and made up of several hundred billion stars, is not alone. Now we know that there are about fifty billion galaxies in principle, visible to the best modern telescopes though as yet only a few thousand have been studied in any detail. This means that there are a minimum of ten thousand billion stars in the visible universe, of which our sun is just one. Hubble also discovered a means of measuring how fast the universe is expanding and also how long since the originating fireball of the Big Bang. Our eyes were really opened then in the 1960s with the discovery of cosmic microwave background radiation, the echo of the Big Bang itself.

Our context is 13.7 billion years old and light years wide. We now have approximate dates and a direction to follow. Cosmologists believe that they know what our universe was like a few seconds after its beginning. The temperature was 10 billion degrees: radiation, protons, neutrons and 'dark matter' were present everywhere in known proportions. However, we still don't know, for instance, what went bang and why the universe was set up to expand in this way, and with this particular mix of ingredients. In this respect, however, science is our ally. It opens doors for us into the mysterious and what earlier generations must have considered unknowable. There is a reductionist view of science that grants reality only to what is measurable. But there is a way of doing science that is more inclusive – a holistic way that does not reject intuitive understandings of God and creation as found in the metaphor and parable of sacred texts. If St Thomas Aquinas were alive today he would be reflecting on the issues raised by contemporary scientific discovery – as he did so memorably in the thirteenth century – and writing a new theology in that awareness. His example invites us to do for our age what he did for his.

The new story of creation is not a fairytale; it is not 'new' as meaning the latest version. It is based on what we have reliably and verifiably come to know through the sciences and, with particular illumination, through those magical instruments, the microscope and telescope. As Chet Raymo observes: 'Only the New Story has the global authority to help us navigate the future … Of all the stories, it is the only one that has had its feet held to the fire of exacting empirical experience.'[2]

This new understanding of the cosmos that science has revealed to us changes everything. New questions follow. We may well be made in the image of God, but the stuff of our being originates from exploding stars. And what of our earth? John Gribbin and Simon Goodwin in *Origins: Our Place in Hubble's Universe*, describe it in this way:

> One of the planets that formed from the swirling disk of dust around the young Sun was just the right distance from the Sun for oceans of liquid water to form and provide a home for life. But every step in the chain, from the Big Bang to life on Earth, depended on the previous step. We are what we are because the Universe is the way it is.[3]

Despite our wonderful abilities of understanding, articulating and making, we are nonetheless inseparably part of the original flourishing, as this poem of mine suggests:

Like it is
In Waterstone's I saw the universe
in a book. Lovely it was to look at
with all those stars and planets and smudges
of dissolving whiteness where a careless sleeve
had reached across the wet.

To think we came from that; that
we were there from the beginning as sequinned
glitter, mother of pearl, bright teardrops
squeezed from black, or homelier, as milk
spill where the cow had kicked back.

Further questions arise. Who are we to bear the burden of witness to this unfolding? What does it demand of us? Is there an Eden ahead? How, and with whom, should we celebrate our being-here? Where is God in all this? And how does this Creator-God speak to us in Jesus?

Our first response must be to deepen our awareness of the

range of relationships implied by a telling of the new story of creation. The right relations it implies must be grounded in a wise practice as expressing our commitment to the planet that we share with other creatures and are learning to love with a new desperation. More tellingly, what we are learning to love is our own place. We realise that the earth is not given to us in a single, global sameness, but articulates itself into bioregions with mutually supporting life systems. In other words, there is an inescapable particularity to our being here.

In a Eucharistic setting, this local frame of reference is our context for sharing the *Shalom* moment of 'peace be with you' with the extended members of the family. This greeting is reciprocated. The region responds to the attention it receives from the various members of the community, just as a performer will respond to a listening audience. This level of sharing is advanced as we work to create a mutually enhancing mode of human dwelling on the earth. St Paul makes use of a metaphor in his description of Christian community that we might extend for our purpose. He writes:

> God has established a harmony in the body, giving special honour to that which needed it most. There was to be no want of unity in the body; all the different parts of it were to make each other's welfare their common care. If one part is suffering, all the rest suffer with it; if one part is treated with honour, all the rest find pleasure in it (1 Cor 12:24b, 25-26).

It becomes an even richer evocation when applied to the whole working out of creation where there is 'no want of unity'. The statement is also striking in sounding a warning to us that we now know to be empirically true: 'If one part is suffering, all the rest suffer with it.'

Living with Gaia

In the late 1960s, James Lovelock found a name for his developing theory that the living planet regulates its atmosphere. The name he adopted, at the suggestion of his friend William Golding, was *Gaia*, after the ancient Greek goddess of the Earth. In essence, his Gaia hypothesis, now Gaia theory, (emphasising the self-regulating abilities of the biosphere interacting with the material environment), seemed to show the totality of life working, as it were, for the common good. But harmony needs to be strictly defined in the scientific establishment and Lovelock had many objectors. From the geologists who found his ideas unnecessary, to the biologists who felt that this planetary conspiracy was all too cosy, raised as they were on the idea of 'nature red in tooth and claw'. Formidable opposition also came from the Darwinians like Richard Dawkins and W. Ford Doolittle for whom balance in nature can only mean a balance between essentially hostile forces, 'constantly probing for chinks in one another's armour or, more generally, looking for a larger share of limited resources.'[4]

The development of Gaia over thirty years makes interesting reading. It is clear that Lovelock's original intuition has proved to be wonderfully productive (for example, in the development of Earth System Science) and has helped shape the way we think about, and relate to, our Earth. Within the scientific community it has now found almost universal support. Against the ideological stance of the neo-Darwinians, Mary Midgley points out (along with many biologists) that competition can only take place on a basis of underlying co-operation; and furthermore, 'such co-operation is in fact found among organisms at all levels, down to the harmonious working of the organelles inside our cells, which were originally separate creatures.'[5] At a meeting in Amsterdam in 2001 more than a thousand scientists, representing the four principal global-change organisations, signed a declaration which began: 'The Earth System behaves as a single, self-regulating system comprised of physical, chemical, biological and human components.'[6] Gaia was now official. True, the scientists didn't get as far as stating that the goal of self-regulating Earth was to 'sustain habitability', but at least there was acceptance of a working model for the Earth. Now the hard work starts. The way we are living is making us unwelcome on the planet. In his latest book, *The Revenge of Gaia*, Lovelock states: 'Unless we see the Earth as a planet that behaves as if it were alive, at least to the extent of regulating its climate and chemistry, we will lack the will to change our way of life and to understand that we have made it our greatest enemy.'[7]

To an objection posed against a universal harmony that is too idealistic, Thomas Berry replies:

> Is the universe ultimately destructive or creative? Violent or co-operative? The mystery is that both extremes are found together. We even find it difficult to determine when violence is simply destructive or when violence is linked to creativity.[8]

When a female spider consumes her mate, he presents, by way of example, is this destruction on her part or is it co-operation on his? And how do we read the behaviour of the offspring of the mother beetle *Micromalthus debilis* which, while still in its larval form, will devour the mother? He points out that violence and destruction are dimensions of the universe and are present at every level of existence: the elemental, the geological, the organic, the human. In this latter regard, our violent nature, as expressed in the casual cruelty of children on their way from Sunday school, is more disconcerting to us than our ongoing war on Gaia. This poem of mine alludes to our indifference to the suffering of fellow creatures and, by inference, to the living Earth.

Natural History
It could have been a bat our of hell
unable to struggle out of its parachute
to the girls from St Mary's chittering
in the quiet, notebook in hand as they stood by
Plecotus Auritus – the pricked ears regal,
wide eyes pleading, 'break the glass, undo the pins' –

like neophytes gazing at the crucified,
those children on their way from Sunday school
trapping the green frogs
whose wriggling bodies they would later nail,
ankle and wrist, to little crosses
while the boy with a pellet gun closed an eye.

We need to move towards a more refined understanding of creation and of the responsibility our species has been given within it. Because of our conventional way of looking at the natural world, we can be blind to both its beauty and brutality. The primitive responses of astonishment and horror can lie dormant in us. In our celebration of Eucharist we may need to learn that the concept of community requires something more of us than our superficial concern with sameness and correctness suggests. The new harmonies of a community of all living beings may not be as melodic as the old; the rhyming schemes of a new religious poetry only partial, if at all.

The world is a communion of subjects, not a collection of objects
There is a story to be told of the origins of the universe, of stars and supernovae (exploding stars), of the emergence of planet Earth, of the beginnings of life, of our own species arriving a relatively short time ago. Thomas Berry, in particular, following on from Teilhard de Chardin's understanding of 'holy matter', has helped us to hear that story in its wholeness. Not only to hear it but to be challenged to act on it in the manner outlined by Jesus' reply, 'My mother and my brothers are those who hear the word of God and put it into practice' (Lk 8:21). For Berry, the universe is the primary sacred reality, the first page of revelation. Pope Benedict concurs: 'The first visible sign of divine love is found in creation.' Even before discovering the God who reveals himself in history, he says, there is the cosmic revelation laid open to us all. 'Secretly inscribed in creation,' we find signs of the 'loving fidelity of God who gives his creatures being and life, water and food.'[9] In this way, the word of God addresses us through myriad modes of presence, from the tiniest organism to the highest mountain. It invites us to stand in awe and wonder at our responsibilities as the uniquely reflective species that we are. Looking at our response in terms of our technological achievements, however, Berry remarks:

> This new world of automobiles, highways, parking lots, shopping malls, power stations, nuclear-weapons plants, factory farms, chemical plants … has become an affliction perhaps greater than the more natural human condition it seeks to replace. We live in a chemical-saturated world. It is not a life-giving situation … We no longer see the stars with the clarity that once existed.[10]

We do not know our own place as numinous reality. If we did, how could we go on despoiling our home, destroying the precise environment we need to sustain our kind of life? The words of Joni Mitchell's song, *Big Yellow Taxi*, seem more ominous thirty five years on: 'Don't it always seem to go / that you don't know what you've got 'til it's gone. / They paved Paradise and put up a parking lot.' Our claim to being 'special' (and closer to God?) must come in for scrutiny. If being 'special' means that we imagine our having arrived from somewhere else and under our own steam, then, inevitably, we will see ourselves as distanced from other living beings. Furthermore, if we see ourselves as heading for a glorious future apart from nature, the impression persists that our being here is more like an audition for the real thing. A theology of hope must include the whole creation.

Central to an understanding of the universe story is our place within it. We are neither addendum nor intrusion but quintessentially integral with the universe. So much so, that the story of the universe over billions of years is our sacred story. So much so indeed, that 'the eye that searches the Milky Way galaxy is itself an eye shaped by the Milky Way. The mind that searches for contact with the Milky Way is the very mind of the Milky Way galaxy in search of its inner depths.'[11] Should we not perhaps add that the life, death and resurrection of Jesus is not distinct from the life, death and resurrection of the living universe of which he is a representative part because the Son of the eternal Father had his origins, too, in that explosion of a seed of infinite energy? Further, that in his awareness of being 'Son' the whole universe celebrates such intimacy? That in his offering of his life to the Father of all creation, all creation is offering itself through him?

A key point for Berry is how our evolving life-story sheds light on our relationships. His challenge to view the world not 'as a collection of objects' but as 'a communion of subjects' calls for a paradigm shift on our part.[12] We have always known that we are related, instinctively, intuitively to every living being though our ancestors lived closer to this truth. In spite of this, there exists at an institutional level, a radical discontinuity between the nonhuman and the human with all the rights and inherent values given to us. Strange that our corporate selves can persist with this view given what we now know: that all life shares a common ancestry, that we are all (including plants, bacteria and fungi) genetically (not just metaphorically) related. Occasionally as individuals, we may feel that affinity as guilt for the careless speed of our lives. These lines of mine arose from such an experience.

Accident
You may never have the recognition
that sits with the criminal-type,
inventive hit-man, bleak sadist
who paws the victim, toys with it,

but remember the spring thrush
that hopped from the hedgerow
into your speeding path –
you must settle out of court for that!

To lay hold of the phrase, 'a community of subjects', is a good beginning. But just that. To invest in what lies behind these words will require that we make a journey – the journey into encounter. To truly encounter another creature will take time, attention and a willingness to be addressed in another language. The voice may sound alien to us because our senses are now so under-used. We are oblivious to other forms of communication, (meaning the chemical alphabet of most living beings), and live, in practice, as if nature were a collection of objects.

I have a memory of boyhood holidays spent with grandparents in Ballyneale, Co Kilkenny. My grandfather was creamery manager at the creamery, (Ida), and his house was hardly a hundred metres away. For two weeks every year, the creamery, with its intoxicating smell of milk, was the centre of our world – from the clip-clop of the horse and cart carrying churns in the morning to the quiet that descended each evening. Perhaps, I should say 'ascended' for this rich and textured silence was there all day long under the noise. What arose at six o'clock with the dying machines was birdsong and wind-song and cattle and voices from far away. But other things, too – coded messages from the countryside that entered me without my knowing. For reasons beyond me, what rose up was completely satisfying –

lonely, to begin with, then reassuring. I was alive.

I use that memory now as a metaphor for how we grow up to live under the tyranny of thought. The thinking machines run on and on until our senses are sidelined with only ever a late call onto the field of play. Without a conscious return to our senses, we cannot take seriously this evocative phrase, 'communion of subjects'. When confronted with an insect or a flower my question more is likely to be, 'what is that?' than 'who are you?' To meet the 'who' requires our being alone and trusting our senses again. It will have to be deliberate, because the 'what' question dominates. It will take time to return to the real fare of communion when our living has become a thin gruel of incessant thinking. But it can be done. Our willingness to do so underpins everything to be said here about Eucharist and creation. I am reminded of two lines I wrote many years ago when I first stood as teacher in a classroom. The bright day ran like honey outside but there was a curriculum to follow.

De-Schooling
Attention!
Today we will finish creation!

The loss of a rich sensory life leaves us lonely and cut off from other beings, our companions, who have a story to tell. The story we have to tell in our Eucharist is that we belong together. When we suffer we suffer together, when we give worship, we worship as one. Adapting the great Shema prayer of Israel, these are words to be told diligently to our children when we sit down together or walk by the way, when we lie down and when we rise.

Love in its cosmic dimension
The phrase, 'a communion of subjects', might be considered a short-hand for the three governing themes of an emerging universe, namely:

 differentiation without which the universe would collapse into a homogeneous smudge;

 self-articulation for in the universe to be is to be different;

 and *communion* where nothing is itself without everything else.[13]

While these terms are used in a descriptive sense, we can also read them as value statements integral to the story of creation. As such, they question how we treat not only fellow humans, but how we relate to all forms of life. Instead of the constant differentiation associated with the evolutionary process, our modern world is directed towards monocultures and standardisation. Against the second, you find that there is little appreciation of the sacred depth of the individual of any species. The third cosmological imperative, that the entire universe is bonded together, is violated when we place our species outside a shared sacred history.

Seen in this light, Eucharist means embracing difference, respecting the integrity of every living being, and modelling, in sacramental terms, a cosmic communion. When our recitation of the Our Father is informed by these themes, it becomes an all-encompassing prayer. 'Thy kingdom come' can then be understood in terms of our shared dream of fulfilment. 'Deliver us from evil' can speak against the ongoing destruction of our shared living quarters; and specifically, a 'deliverance' of our species from its exploitative self. For we can no longer think of the sacrificial death of Jesus (and the presence of sacrifice entailed in a burgeoning universe) without a care for the wanton destruction of habitat or the extinction of species. In a Spirit-filled universe, we must acknowledge that the One who made such coastal friends of thrift and sea campion also made us! Acknowledge, too, that the bread and wine, fruits of the earth, are to be honoured long before the invocation of the Spirit brings about a new reality through them for us, namely, the risen Jesus. In their greenness, they embody the sun (our sacred heart!) which converts 700 million tons of hydrogen to helium to give us light and heat each second. There is a giving at the heart of creation expressed in such processes which calls us to bend the knee and bow our heads, knowing ourselves to be utterly blessed. When Teilhard reflects on the image of the Sacred Heart as a furnace of fire, he sees the contours of Christ's body melt away to be transformed into 'the face of a world that has burst into flame'.[14] In the heart of the Fire is love.

At the heart of our stupendous universe is an allurement that calls into being and creates community. To call it 'gravity' – as if in explanation – fails to do justice to its mysterious presence. It could be described as love in its cosmic dimension. It ranges from lovers in each other's arms to stars in their galactic dance. In Brian Swimme's words:

This primal dynamism awakens the communities of atoms, galaxies, stars, families, nations, persons, ecosystems, oceans and stellar systems. Love ignites being ... (Without it) all interest, enchantment, fascination, mystery and wonder would fall away, and with their absence all human groups would lose their binding energy.[15]

This alluring activity reigns on every level, happily for us in the Earth's attraction to the sun. In this bonding, too, love ignites being. We need to welcome such connections. Cardinal Ratzinger, now Pope Benedict, advises:

Christians look toward the east, the rising sun. This is not a case of Christians worshipping the sun but of the cosmos speaking of Christ. The song of the sun in Psalm 19 is interpreted as a song about Christ when it says: '[The sun] comes forth like a bridegroom leaving his chamber ... Its rising is from the end of the heavens, and its circuit to the end of them' (vv 5f).[16]

For the early church this was the real Christmas psalm – Christ the true sun of history coming forth in Bethlehem from the Virgin Mary to enlighten the whole world. Indeed, the dates assigned for celebrating Christ's incarnation, cross and resurrection are connected so intimately with the earth's relationship to the sun that their cosmic significance is obvious. Even the feast of John the Baptist on June 24 at the time of the summer solstice is linked to the feasts of Christ's conception (March 25) and his birth (December 25). The Baptist's birthday takes place when the days begin to shorten, the Saviour's when they begin again to lengthen, giving liturgical and cosmic expression to the words, 'He (Christ) must increase, but I must decrease' (Jn 3:30). Such a reading might seem fanciful to us, but the former Cardinal points out that we have good reason to 'take on the challenge of the sun cult and incorporate it positively into the theology of the Christmas feast.'[17] From this day the light advances while the night retreats. An older tradition presents Ezekiel's recurring vision of God's 'glory' filling the Temple in the grandeur of the rising sun. 'The angel took me to the gate, the one facing east. I saw the glory of the God of Israel approaching from the east ... and the earth shone with his glory' (43: 1-3). The design of the monstrance used for Eucharistic benediction speaks of the risen Jesus as the light of the world. He is the rising sun whose rays reach out to all creatures. Through the window of the sacred Host comes in the wonder of creation. In his homily for the Feast of Corpus Christi, 2006, the Holy Father catches that nuance when he states: 'When, in adoration, we look at the consecrated Host, the sign of creation speaks to us.'[18] (It is noteworthy that our date for Easter depends on the dalliance of sun and moon. Easter Sunday is the first Sunday after the full moon after the spring equinox.)

The story of the Universe is our sacred story

One of the difficulties we face is how to present this 'dream of the earth' as our story, in such a way that it may evoke admiration and awe and an urge to give praise. In a wonderful essay, *How The Camel Got His Hump*, Alan Lightman draws our attention to two different ways of telling a story. He does so by describing an occasion of putting his daughter to bed. She wants to hear how the magic Djinn in charge of All Deserts could cause the camel's back to puff up suddenly. In answer to her question as to the usefulness of the hump anyway, he explains how the hump is made of fat and how the camel stores all its fat in one place so he can cool off more easily. Nature took billions of years, he explains tendentiously, to design him like that. At the end of it all, 'Daddy,' she says, 'will you read to me again about the Djinn and how he made the hump puff up with magic?'[19] In just three pages he makes such an important point. Besides the precise and exciting knowledge that science offers, we must also incorporate it in a way that is artistically, or imaginatively, true. Poetry and story will help here, as will other art forms, as will ritual. These are not attempts to spiritualise or sentimentalise reality but to present it to our imagination in a compelling way. A striking exemplar of this is James Lovelock. His personification of the complexity of systems which regulate the Earth as Gaia makes for an emotional response. His metaphor helps us find the music in the story. A scientific account alone does not command the fullness of human response. The world of advertising knows this and uses remarkable ingenuity to gloss the most ordinary product as a key to happiness. Our story must entrance, which means it must be true at many levels, if it is to become the basis of a new global ethic where relationships are characterised by respect for diversity and for the integrity of each individual, where communion takes precedence over competition.

Rachel Carson, in *Silent Spring*, begins in this way. 'There was once a town in the heart of America where all life seemed to live in harmony with its surroundings ... with fields of grain and hillsides of orchards where, in spring, white clouds of bloom drifted above the green fields.' She describes then how 'some evil spell' came to settle on the community, with illness and death spreading everywhere. 'There was a strange stillness. The birds, for example – where had they gone? ... The feeding stations in the backyards were deserted. The few birds seen anywhere were moribund; they trembled violently and could not fly. It was a spring without voices.'[20] Written in 1962, her remarkable story is borne out with incontrovertible evidence of the destruction caused by the pesticides, insecticides and herbicides sprayed with abandon in a world urged to beat its ploughshares into spray guns. Her recounting of the wild flowers and shrubs under threat from roadside brush control as reported by botanists in Connecticut reads like a sacred litany.

> Azaleas, mountain laurel, blueberries, huckleberries, viburnums, dogwood, bayberry, sweet fern, low shadbush, winterberry, chokeberry and wild plum are dying before the chemical barrage. So are the daisies, black-eyed Susans, Queen Anne's lace, goldenrods, and autumn asters which lend grace and beauty to the landscape.[21]

She insinuates the moral question rather than preaches it, by presenting the evidence. She speaks of the supreme arrogance of 'ruling over nature' for, quoting Dr Briejer, 'Life is a miracle beyond our comprehension, and we should reverence it even where we have to struggle against it.'[22] As Linda Lear says of her: 'she deplored ... the cultural tendency to see the nature world as little more than an aggregate of impersonal commodities, rather than an integrated, organic and living whole'[23] For Carson environmental destruction is a

> problem of ecology, of interrelationships, of interdependence. We poison the caddis flies in a stream and the salmon runs dwindle and die. We poison the gnats in a lake and the poison travels from link to link of the food chain and soon the birds of the lake margins become its victims. We spray our elms and the following springs are silent of robin song, not because we sprayed the robins directly but because the poison travelled, step by step, through the now familiar elm leaf-earthworm-robin cycle.[24]

With prophetic daring she managed to waken a whole generation to the intricate web of life whose interwoven strands lead from microbes to man. In many ways, she has left us a work in progress, with the invitation, 'Now, over to you.' Given what we now know of our mutual involvement with every living thing, it's hard to hear Christ's words, 'I have come that they may have life and have it in abundance' (Jn.10:10), and seem unconcerned about what militates against it. To weaken by indiscriminate spraying the community of the soil with its life-giving bacteria, threadlike fungi, algae, mites, springtails and the extraordinary earthworm is to cast scorn on the scriptural word. When it comes to celebrating Eucharist and offering 'the fruits of the earth', we can hardly leave these minute creatures and their contribution to our well being out of the story. It is their sacred story, too.

How to make room in our liturgies for sorrowing Mother Earth
It is to cherish something essential to our Eucharistic celebration to place it explicitly within our growing understanding of the evolutionary process – to ritualise our oneness with all creation. We might then acknowledge that to celebrate Eucharist is to gather all of life together as represented in the fruit of the plants of the earth. We would recall that at the heart of the Eucharist is the action of Jesus on his knees washing feet. That reverence we would assume is directed towards every creature, irrespective of the number of feet, or its particular arrangement of stamens

and carpels. We might suggest that the bread and wine is not added to, but in the extension of hands over it, its deepest relationship to us is insisted upon – namely, that our survival from day to day is dependent on plants. Jesus seems to have wanted his memory to be associated with such intimacy. Our plea to the Spirit then that we may all be one will include the insects, the mammals, the birds of the air who feed as we do from the nourishment of sunlight broken for us by the plants. For Eucharist is in the awareness of thanks to all, to the One in whom all is one, with no exception. It is meant as a moment of such insight; in the Eucharist we are nourished into oneness with all creation as Jesus' memory proclaims.

The global ethic that follows from the cosmic dimension of the Eucharist will require this kind of compelling storyline if it is to cut deep enough. We want to go deeper than a romantic feeling about nature, for life also has its bitter and burdensome aspects at all levels. With a new articulation, the great religions have much to offer if they can hear the cries of earth expressed in the estrangement of the poor and endangered, if they can make room in their liturgies for Gaia, the sorrowing Mother Earth. The image of Mary standing by the Cross comes to mind. Rather than weakening her role as mother of him through whom all things were made by making this connection, it highlights her maternal relationship with the whole of suffering creation. On this point eco-feminists are quite clear in connecting the oppression of women with the unbridled abuse of our household, Earth. They point to the hierarchical dualism at work in much patriarchal thinking, aligning men with culture, for example, and women with nature. As a strategy, women with this understanding side with nature as a way of re-claiming their inherent dignity and the dignity of the natural world. They read environmental issues as issues of justice and point persuasively to the imbalance of power in gender relations. In many countries the power differential is so great that women can be used and abused without redress, their ill-treatment a metaphor for the way we often abuse the natural world.

A Eucharistic spirituality must accommodate the ecological wisdom of women. Of course, special mention is always given to Mary, the mother of Jesus, as the woman 'who sings of the "new heavens" and the "new earth" ' (*EE*, par 58). Yet we take less seriously its far-reaching consequences: namely, that in every celebration of the Eucharist 'the seeds of that new history wherein the mighty are "put down from their thrones" and "those of low degree are exalted" take root in the world' (idem). As a statement of Christian hope, her Magnificat can enliven our ecological concerns as we recognise a universe seeded with promise. Our own longing for future fulfilment blossoms in that shared promise expressed in terms of 'new heavens' and 'new earth' when God will be all in all. As Eucharistic people, this must become our dream and plan of action so that Christ's tumbling of the walls dividing Jews from Gentiles – men from women, rich from poor, human from non-human – to make of them 'one body', be not in vain (Eph 2:14-16). It asks for conversion, not as a simple return to good practice but as an opening up, as Vatican II suggested, a coming to our senses with the fresh air of the Spirit on our faces and the voices of creation in our ears.

'Where he is, the elands are in droves like cattle'
Our new story of creation deserves the best of storytellers – teachers, spiritual people, poets and scientists, grandmothers and fathers – for the story will need a different articulation in different Eucharistic settings drawing on different kinds of wisdom. The wisdom of indigenous peoples, for instance.'Where did Coti, the wife of Kaggen, come from?' asks J. M. Orpen in 1873 of Qing, a San speaker from the Maluti mountains in South Africa, who replies: 'I don't know, perhaps with those who brought the sun; but you are now asking the secrets that are not spoken of ... only the initiated men of that dance know these things.' To his question, 'Where is the trickster deity, Kaggen – the creator of the eland?' she replies: 'We do not know but the elands do. Have you not hunted and heard his cry, when the elands suddenly start and run to his call? Where he is, the elands are in droves like cattle' (Text on display in the Natural History Museum, Cape Town, SA).

The beauty of the poetry is infused by her reverence for the secrets of life and the honesty of her, 'I don't know.' Krishnamurti, the great spiritual teacher, explains that there is a true humility in the 'I don't know' which is 'always in a state of learning without ever accumulating.'[25] This is the attitude of those who approach the Eucharist in hope as the ineffable God in communion with us. It is interesting that Rublev's famous icon of the Trinity places the Eucharist, the homely image of a shared meal, within that mystery. In contrast, we have at times been so anxious to protect its truth that we have encased the Eucharist in dogmatic words and phrases, then used them as tools of ownership. In a world that is endlessly surprising, why do we limit ourselves to habits of thought, old formulations, and neglect 'another duty, that of examining and prudently bringing forth "things new" (cf Mt 13:52).'[26] Strangely, it is scientific discovery that often leads us back to the 'amazement' proper to authentic worship. Its wisdom is not to be ignored.

A detail of exact knowledge, for example, rather than an appeal to sentiment, can rouse us to wonder. When you hear that there are two hundred and twenty eight separate and distinct muscles in the head of a caterpillar, you want to hear more. It's quite possible to spend a lifetime trying to get to know just one species and many people do. To know any wild 'other' in any depth calls for a profound attentiveness. Even an incomplete description of the 'waggle dance' of the honeybee an elaborate dance performed in the hive (in the dark!) to inform the others of newly discovered flower patches and their exact location some distance away, is mind-boggling. In our limited way, we describe it as symbolic language. Over and over the bee traces a line on the vertical surface of the comb. To return to the starting line she loops back first to the right and then to the left making a figure-eight, waggling her abdomen all the while and emitting a high-pitched buzz. The sister workers crowd in close. Taken together, the energy, duration and direction of her movements, and other forms of communication unknown to us, convey the distance to the food supply (even up to three miles away) and its abundance. If she dances straight upwards on the comb the food is to be found in the direction of the sun. If she goes fifteen degrees to the right of vertical, it is to be found fifteen degrees to the right of the sun. This discovery by Karl von Frisch in 1923 brought him a Nobel Prize and brought a sliver of understanding to us of the utter complexity of another species. It should be noted that all species commune. In recent years, the discovery of sophisticated communication even in bacteria, using an alphabet of chemical signals, serves to further question human presumption. It becomes clear that we are part of an unbelievable communion. We have an amazing story to tell.

As humans, we have an ability to empathise imaginatively with others, to recognise their inwardness and give thanks for it. The Eucharistic thanksgiving sends us out to share the bread of life with all creation and to enter into communion with the least of his brothers and sisters (Mt 25:40). To do so, is to become fully who we are because we have found a good depth of soil in ourselves and can say, 'This is my home.' In John McGahern's novel, *That they may Face the Rising Sun*, Joe Ruttledge has returned from England with his wife to find a new life for themselves. In answer to the auctioneer's question, 'What do you find wrong with England?', Ruttledge replies: 'Nothing but it's not my country and I never feel it's quite real or that my life there is real. That has it's pleasant side as well. You never feel responsible or fully involved in anything that happens. It's like being present and at the same time a real part of you is happily absent.'[27] Perhaps this is our unexamined attitude to the ground on which we stand. Maybe we consider ourselves exiles in a foreign land and so can excuse ourselves for a divil-may-care attitude. But 'home is not a creation of sentimentality, it is a creation of fact,' writes Krishnamurti, '– the fact that I feel at home … Total responsibility is the feeling of being at home.'[28] In the corroborative words of the encyclical (*EE*): the Christian vision of 'new heavens' and 'a new earth' (Rev 21:1) is not meant as an escape route from our own place but 'increases, rather than lessens, our sense of responsibility for the world today' (par 20). John Feehan's poem, *October Poem 1972*, says it memorably:

> i am filled with trust
> at all that is, charged with trust
> for all that is, unto dust,
> dust of the desert's rock, dust of the way,
> dust of my own decay.
>
> thou knowest o lord these bones can live.

and indeed I shall always feel
there is nothing to give but my nothingness
until I can commune with leaves, no
words to utter but my wordlessness
before ripples on rocks, and autumn's mystery
striking my soul from his horse.[29]

CHAPTER THREE

The implications of an ecological conversion for our celebration of the Eucharist

Yet sometimes when the sun comes through a gap
These men know God the Father in a tree;
The Holy Spirit is the rising sap,
And Christ will be the green leaves that will come
At Easter from the sealed and guarded tomb.[1]

On 17 January 2001, Pope John Paul II made this statement:
Mankind, especially in our time, has without hesitation dev-
astated wooded plains and valleys, polluted waters, disfig-
ured the earth's habitat, made the air unbreathable, disturbed
the hydrogeological and atmospheric spheres, turned luxuri-
ant areas into deserts and undertaken forms of unrestrained
industrialisation, humiliating the flower-garden of the universe, to use the image of Dante Aligheri (*Paradiso*, XXII, 151).

In effect, 'the Creator's steward' has turned 'autonomous despot
who is finally beginning to understand that he must stop at the
edge of the abyss.'[2] This state of affairs, he concludes, can only
be redressed by an 'ecological conversion'. It is timely to hear a
clarion call from such an authority, as there is a perception
among Christians that environmental matters are not the business of faith. (The omission of this important talk of the Holy
Father from the *Compendium of the Social Doctrine of the Church,*
2004 is baffling.[3])The former Cardinal Ratzinger indirectly addresses this misperception in his robust defence of our turning
towards the east, towards the rising sun, as 'the permanent orientation' of the Christian liturgy.

Are we not interested in the cosmos any more? Are we today
really hopelessly huddled in our own little circle? Is it not important, precisely today, to pray with the whole of creation?
Is it not important, precisely today, to find room for the dimension of the future?[4]

The ramifications of this cosmic dimension are significant. Conversion has always been a core value of Christianity but to widen its embrace to include our relationship with the natural world and with the future must give cause for optimism. It reminds us that our love for all creation 'is not to be just words or mere talk, but something real and active' (1 Jn 3:18).

There is no clear connection expressed, however, between an ecological conversion and our Eucharistic celebration, though making such a connection is of the utmost importance. Certainly, the Holy Father does not do so but it does not seem unreasonable to combine his call for an ecological conversion and his desire 'to rekindle this Eucharistic "amazement"' (*EE*, par 6). His reference to the Eucharist as being always 'in some way celebrated on the altar of the world' leads naturally on to a consideration of the 'fitness' of that altar, its state of health, its integrity, its sacredness. In the encyclical (*EE*), and in the companion Apostolic Letter (*MND*) the concern is 'to banish the dark clouds of unacceptable doctrine and practice, so that the Eucharist will shine forth in all its radiant mystery' (*EE*, par 10). The 'radiant mystery' must also be allowed to express its 'cosmic character'; to be set not under a tub but 'on a lamp-stand where it shines for everyone in the house' (Mt 5:14 and Jn 8:12). Only when this connection is made with creation can the Eucharist truly shed light on our being in the world, and our being in the world shed light on our understanding of the Eucharist.

This new knowledge of the universe unfolding from the beginning through the formation of its first stars to the formation of our own sun, some 4.5 billion years ago is staggering. And then we think of our own solar system being formed from material partially processed inside two or more generations of preceding stars and are amazed at the beauty of the story. Amazed to find ourselves on an ordinary planet orbiting an ordinary star in a smaller than average galaxy, one of tens of billions of galaxies in the Universe. Edward O. Wilson's comment is appropriate here when he says:

> A change of heart occurs when people look beyond themselves to others, and then to the rest of life. It is strengthened when they also expand their view of landscape, from parish

to nation and beyond, and their sweep of time from their own life spans to multiple generations and finally to the extended future history of mankind.[5]

We must assume it is along these lines that an 'ecological conversion', as a new relationship with creation, becomes possible. It is along these lines also that 'the breadth and the length, the height and the depth,' of Christ's love is to be considered (Eph 3:19). His cosmic love which we share in the Eucharist reconciles 'everything in heaven and everything on earth' (Col 1:20). It should not be forgotten that to this day God's covenant relationship with all creation – 'birds, cattle, every wild beast' – is writ large for us in a rainbow-haloed sky (Gen 9:17).

The world is not there solely for us
There are obstacles to this change of mind and heart. Firstly, flowing from our belief in our exalted place in the world. As psalm 35 has it: 'he so flatters himself in his mind/ that he knows not his guilt ... / All wisdom is gone'. The first and fundamental stage of conversion must begin with the dawning realisation that the world is not there solely for us. We have been taught to regard the earth and its colour and fruitfulness as a gift from the Creator to his favourite species; taught to regard this planet as a toy tossed into the playpen of a childish race to be kicked around. The idea of the passing world reinforced this notion, with its stark reminder that this was not our true home. It was more like rented accommodation that one was dissuaded from investing in, giving rise as it did to 'the sensual body, the lustful eye, pride in possessions' (1 Jn 2:15-17). We were to look heavenwards, recognising that we were a cut above the rest of un-thinking, unconscious creation; the myriad non-human species being no more than sources of food/medicine for us, or, at best, an example of the intelligent creator's artful design. Despite the flaw of Original Sin, we occupied top spot. God surely loved us more than any other species and had plans for our future happiness. After all, the Son of God was one of us.

'Ecological conversion' will mean a radical shift in our religious thinking. To accord citizenship to the tiniest form of life will be a challenge to the most Christian democrat. To take our place with the plant and animal world and know ourselves as part of it will call for a scaling down of our ambition. The poet, Patrick Kavanagh, had the measure of his contemporaries when he wrote in self-parody:

He had the knack of making men feel
As small as they really were
Which meant as great as God had made them
But as males they disliked his air.[6]

He detested the arrogance of the high-and-mighty and the bluff and bluster that passes for superiority, what e. e. cummings ridicules as the posturing of 'this fine specimen of hypermagical ultra omnipotence'.[7] A child experiences the created world as an adventure. Being a part of it all astonishes him. Later, sadly, he becomes Narcissus, staring into the still water of his own reflection, enraptured by his own image, in which he drowns.

In the pastoral document, *Gaudium et Spes* of Vatican II, we find our special status described as follows: 'This likeness (to the divine Persons) reveals that man, who is the only creature on earth *which God willed for itself,* cannot fully find himself except through a sincere gift of himself' (art 24), (italics mine).[8] Further, 'he is master of all earthly creatures that he might subdue them and use them to God's glory' (art 12), as 'God intended the earth and all that it contains for the use of every human being and people' (art 69). *The Catechism of the Catholic Church* (1994) supports this prevailing attitude where it says that the work of creation is prolonged 'by subduing the earth, both with and for one another' (no 2427).[9] It recalls that 'the seventh commandment enjoins respect for the integrity of creation. Animals, like plants and inanimate beings, are by nature destined for the common good of past, present and future humanity' (no 2415). That same paragraph does qualify its position by stating that 'man's dominion ... is not absolute; ... it requires a religious respect for the integrity of creation.' The latter is as close as one gets to a statement of nature's own inherent rights and sacred dimension. By linking the Christian Sunday with thanksgiving for the gift of creation, however, Cardinal Ratzinger, (now the Holy Father), elaborates on our responsibilities and our need to recognise that 'sin wrecks creation'. He continues:

Subdue (the earth)!'... does not mean: Enslave it! Exploit it! Do with it what you will! No, what it does mean is: Recognise it as God's gift! Guard it and look after it, as sons look after what they have inherited from their father. Look after it, so that it becomes a true garden for God and its meaning is fulfilled, so that for it, too, God is 'all in all'.[10]

While this is the 'good steward' model of relating to the earth, there is an acceptance of a shared eschatological promise given to all creation. In this understanding our special status expresses itself in terms of communion with all creatures, not dominance over them. According to James Lovelock, our relationship with the created world is more accurately described as being, through our intelligence and communication, its nervous system. With deep feeling, he expresses that relationship thus:

Through us Gaia has seen herself from space and seen how beautiful she is, and she begins to know her place in the universe. We should be the mind and heart of the Earth, not its malady. Most of all, we should remember that we are a part of Gaia and it is indeed our home.[11]

There is urgent need of a return to the scriptural Word but with new eyes and ears. Reading the inspiring Word at a Eucharistic celebration from an eco-centric point of view will bring it to life again, just as water given to a parched plant will cause it to revive. The following might be offered as an approach. Taken at random, the scriptural texts offered for the 27th week in Ordinary time (Year A) are Isaiah 5:1-7 and Matthew 21: 33-43. Both take a vineyard and its cultivation as their central image. Reading these passages today surely calls for a different attention. In the first passage the produce is spoiled, in the second the produce is withheld. The resultant destruction of the vineyard is instructive from an ecological perspective. The care of the landowner is stressed in both accounts; the actions of the owner in Isaiah are expressive of 'his love for his vineyard'. In Matthew, the owner plants, fences, digs and builds but the wicked tenants, in attempting to take over the inheritance, throw the owner's son 'out of the vineyard' (where he belongs) and kill him. We can perhaps overhear in this narrative concerns regarding climate change, the pollution of life systems, the greed of multi-nationals, disregard for our shared inheritance. This is the kind of multi-layered reading that needs to become familiar to a Christian congregation, for the Word is proclaimed to challenge our complacency as much as to console.

The parables of Jesus easily accommodate themselves to contemporary concerns. The parable of the sower scattering seed cannot leave us unmoved unless we have completely lost touch with the earth (Mk 4:1-20). The parables that tell of finding what was lost can direct our gaze towards the loss of biodiversity. Treasure hidden in our fields is a reality we are amazingly willing to abandon for easy return. The rejected invitation to a banquet reminds us that the invitation also extends to the poor and to the inhabitants of the open roads and hedgerows. The fine pearls of our lost traditions are replaced by imports and pale imitations. (In a recent story of a wealthy woman who wears fake jewellery because the insurance to protect the original (now lodged in a bank vault) is too expensive, there are echoes of Jesus' warning about bigger barns and burying talents.)

At the table of the Word there might also be opportunities to listen to supplementary readings from some of our environmental prophets who speak to us of hope as well as gloom. At the table of the Eucharist, time to recall those thousands of species we have unthinkingly hurried to extinction as we pray that 'all the departed' may be brought 'into the light of your presence' (Eucharistic Prayer II). And time to consider how 'happy are they who are invited to the wedding supper of the Lamb,' including all his servants, 'small and great' (Rev 19:4-9).

Being attentive to the signs of the times (which is a gospel imperative) must feed into our faith. And signs are everywhere. We must become familiar with the awe-inspiring discoveries of the new cosmology, the environmental problems and issues of our time like global warming, the destruction of the ozone layer, the extinction of natural diversity, overpopulation and our loss of direct contact with the natural world; then commit ourselves to appropriate action as a necessary extension of Eucharistic worship.

This new understanding will be fundamental for any conversion worthy of the name. Something must knock us to the ground and off our high horses. This ground is our home, it is the space we have been allotted to share with the others who were here before us. It is the first page of revelation to be read, preceding as it does the literal word.

We are biologically, not simply metaphorically, related to one another
Humans are members in, and not masters of, the community of life. We are biologically and not simply metaphorically related to one another. Indeed, we are psychically attuned to the heart-beat of nature, so that an experience of the wild will bring us to our senses. The prophet, Hosea, speaks out of that awareness when he attributes this insight to Yahweh and his plans to win back his unfaithful people:

I am going to lure her
And lead her out into the wilderness
And speak to her heart …
There she will respond to me as she did when she was young,
As she did when she came out of the land of Egypt (Hosea 2: 16-17).

As a study of initiation rites attests, it seems good for us to be completely 'bewildered' at some time in our lives. Conversion seems to include such dislocation. St Paul's experience of being thrown from his horse on the road to Damascus leaves him, literally, in the dark. In his blindness, his heart is opened to the Christ he is persecuting. His bewilderment prepares him for the gift of new sight.

I remember as a boy walking in the woods in Heywood, Co Laois and being touched beyond all reasoning by the housed darkness, the company of trees, the adventure and danger of being lost. It was pre-reflective then but now I know that I was being led by the earth-spirits into my own heart. It was home-coming, far beyond home. I was loving it. Nature had introduced herself to me, intimating that what was second nature might again become first. Later, in my early twenties, the wonder of boyhood was restored again in the wild places of the Slieve Blooms. Here was a landscape in which I felt both lost and found. Lost in its wilderness, found as though I had been there before. It seems clear now that the code of our belonging is inscribed in our being and draws us towards the natural world as surely as an insect is drawn to its flower. It is worth noting the ripple of excitement among visitors to the Botanical Gardens in Dublin as they gaze at the recently-arrived Wollemi pine (*Wollemia Nobilis*), dating back 200 million years to the time of the dinosaurs. Thought to have been extinct with only fossil records remaining, its discovery in Sydney's Blue Mountains by David Noble in 1994 re-connects us in a way to the ancestral landscape of our forest home. Our kinship is no longer a matter simply of intuition. We now know not only that we belong, but how (genetically) we belong to the community of life. To take seriously this new evidence, and to trust its implications for human meaning, will require us to bend the knee to this grace-filled ground with an awakened sense of body greeting body.

In the Eucharist we consider the living Christ as being deeply rooted in our experience of the earth, for he has also experienced death and tomb-life, has consorted with the dead and raised them to new life. In this way, death, too, is imbued with meaning. Resurrection is not an escape from death as the empty tomb might suggest. Rather, it upholds the place of death as central to every life (without giving it the last word), so much so that in the Eucharist we celebrate the Paschal Mystery as the 'life, death and resurrection' of Jesus. 'Sister Death,' as Francis of Assisi would say, is no stranger to us. She is family and must be made welcome. The following verse of mine suggests that our being participants in the earth story is never clearer than at the end.

Cousins
Cousins of ours: beech and chestnut,
Still water, rabbits hopping
Out of reach, big boys
Yawning behind bars.

Then the leaves drop off
Singly, or in a shower
And we bury you, a cutting,
As we plant flowers.

Every living thing breathes. All of us share the originating and loving Spirit-Breath of life from bacteria to whale, and especially the trees and green plants which supply us with the oxygen we need to live. From such communion, compassion grows. Indeed, from understanding such compassion directed towards us, communion grows.

Celebrating Eucharist with the Living Earth

There is the ongoing debate as to the 'livingness' of the Earth. The common notion that only organisms have life is questioned convincingly by Stan Rowe in his article 'Earth Alive'. He says that if we adopt an ecological viewpoint, we must see that the ecosystem is the carrier of life rather than its organic parts alone. He goes on:

> Awareness of Earth as the giver and maintainer of life, shifting the focus from organisms to the larger system that is their mutual source and support, might in time revivify and re-enchant a world that science for several hundred years has assumed to be dead.[12]

Only this kind of awareness will enable us to celebrate our Eucharist not only on the earth, but with the Earth. The living Earth on my doorstep thanks you as I do this day. In the celebration where the priest with the priestly people become part of Jesus' offering in that amazing give-and-take of Father, Son and Spirit (cf Rublev's icon), they cannot remain apart from the living Earth in its own thanksgiving. For the psalmist,

> the heavens proclaim the glory of God/ and the firmament shows forth the work of his hands./Day unto day takes up the story/ and night unto night makes known the message./ No speech, no word, no voice is heard,/ yet their span extends through all the earth (Psalm 18).

This transformation of heart and mind does not come easily. There are vested interests in maintaining the status quo. Even churches are slow to speak of nature in terms of numinous presence. Perhaps they see our yearning to be special in some ultimate sense (the *imago Dei*) weakened by sharing 'specialness' with the created world. Or is it the perennial fear of pantheism, the belief inspired by the potency/fertility of nature? Either way, we seem to employ a strategy of dumbing-down the non-human in order to promote ourselves. Yet God saw creation to be 'very good', not necessarily good for us but good in its very being (Gen 1:31). We have need of conversion here, not only from our being special in the sense of being superior and god-like, but in respect of a deeper appreciation towards this sacred place where divine goodness is expressed. The question, 'And who do you think you are?' bears recall at every Christian assembly. It echoes God's address to us in our common infancy narrative: 'Where are you?' meaning 'You have separated yourselves from the rest of my creation' (Gen 3:9). It is high time to heal that split.

The late Holy Father's call for an 'ecological conversion' in 2001 is not well known. Not many Lenten Pastoral Letters have included it. Certainly, there have been, in recent years, some official statements to support a community of life understanding of creation, but nothing to compare with the courageous leadership of the World Council of Churches in highlighting issues of justice and ecology for over thirty years. Only with the encyclical, *Sollicitudo Rei Socialis* (On Social Concern 1988) does the environment make its way to the table of Roman Catholic concerns. In paragraph 34 of that document we find the following:

> The limitations imposed from the beginning by the Creator himself and expressed symbolically by the prohibition 'not to eat of the fruit of the tree' shows clearly enough that, when it comes to the natural world, we are subject not only to biological laws, but also to moral ones, which cannot be violated with impunity.[13]

These moral considerations include a call to respect the genetic integrity of other species, a recognition that limited natural resources must be protected for future generations and an acknowledgement of the negative impact of industrialisation. A more challenging comment is to be found in the Pope's message for World Day of Peace 1990, *Peace with God the Creator, Peace with All Creation,* in which Catholics are reminded that 'their responsibility within creation and their duty towards nature and the Creator are an essential part of their faith'.[14] He might have added 'and of their worship,' given that our responsibility is not only 'towards' creation but arises from 'within' it.

It is obvious that there has been a deficit in official teaching on the inherent rights of the earth. Even in the late Holy Father's *Letter to Artists* (1999), creation is presented as the place of human endeavour and creativity. By being made in the image of God, he says, our task is firstly to shape the 'material' of our own humanity and then exercise 'creative dominion' over the universe. Reflecting on the creation story in Genesis (1:28-31), he says:

> Finally (God) created the human being, the noblest fruit of divine design, to whom he made the visible world subject, as a vast field in which human inventiveness might assert itself.[15]

What appears lacking in his commentary is the awareness that it is we who are 'shaped' by the universe; that our creativity can now be understood as the universe being creative through us. To work *with* the Earth catches the spirit of the new cosmology better than to work *on* the Earth. To view created reality as 'a communion of subjects' is the beginning of a new relationship with the world.

If this is how we want to relate to the earth, then there are implications. What is the Christian attitude to waste disposal, for instance, even waste disposal in space? Since Sputnik was launched in 1957 about 4500 rockets have followed, each generating its own junk, and there are now thought to be tens of millions of pieces of debris in orbit around the Earth. Is waste-management pertinent to our celebration of Eucharist? Can we despoil the earth, its life-systems and its environs and then give praise to the Lord of creation? When Jesus took a little earth and wet it with his spittle to anoint the eyes of the blind man, was he not in some way restoring the man to his native place, to seeing it again with a new respect? When he allowed his body to be broken in death to reconcile Jew and Gentile, is it too much to insist that all divisions, including human and non-human, are reconciled: 'you who used to be far away have been brought near by the death of Christ' (Eph 2:13-16).

An ecological conversion must bear fruit
When we are dismissed at the end of the Eucharist to 'go in peace to love and serve the Lord' there are tasks before us. Among our neighbourly concerns, we might resolve to observe the amount of waste we create and seek to limit it; or examine

our use of the gift of water and inform ourselves about its quality. But, above all, we must look to the reality of food as being central to the Eucharist. At the Eucharistic table the invitation of Jesus is to eat and drink as sacrament of our communion with him and with all creation. The bread of life binds human beings with the nourishing earth, and it binds human community. This does not in any way belittle the *mysterium fidei* of the bread and wine offering themselves to be Christ's body and blood through the action of the Holy Spirit, but acknowledges that Christ's real presence is rooted in earthly realities. In the words of Gerard Manley Hopkins, 'there lives the dearest freshness deep down things'.[16]

The patenting of seeds is another area of special concern for those who eat from the one loaf. We are now aware how First World corporate seed companies can pillage the genetic resources of Third World countries, develop new varieties of seeds and sell them back to their original countries at huge profit. Against this attempted 'ownership' of life, stand the seed-saving organisations as signs of hope. In Mark chapter 4, Jesus offers three 'seed' (growth) parables to describe the kingdom of God: the seed thriving in good soil, the seed sprouting in its own time, and the example of the mustard seed, the smallest of all seeds becoming the greatest of shrubs. In the buried seed is the hope of creation, an image of death and new life which is brought to completion in the Eucharist. There are also issues of justice to consider, 'for I was hungry and you gave me no food.' Or, in an enlarged context, ' I was hungry and you destroyed my habitat; you suffocated the living soil with chemicals. I was thirsty and you polluted the living stream.' 'When you did this to the little ones, you did it to me' (Mt 25:42). Divine presence is not confined to our species alone.

For too long, we have sought out the God of the 'interior' places; we have abandoned the Earth for a God of pure thought. The potter-God of Jeremiah, one suspects, by contrast, is not afraid of clay under his fingernails – 'as the clay is in the potter's hand so you are in mine' (18:6). 'Participation' as our ethical response to the created world appeals for direct contact. It challenges spiritualities that are ego-driven, concerned about saving 'the soul' but with little reference to the planet and to the other species whose survival, like ours, depends on it. An 'ecological conversion' implies a broadening and deepening of who we are. Holiness, it seems to say, lies in the development of an 'ecological self', giving praise to the Lord of creation with every other creature. The production of occasional thematic liturgies on environmental issues, using eco-language or writing a book, for example, do not necessarily imply a broadening and deepening of the self.

In the context of conversion, there is a type of religious practice which merely 'translates' the world into new ideas and paradigms but doesn't go further. Conversion, in this case, stays at the level of concept; it could be caricatured as being concerned with beliefs rather than with faith. Indeed, the whole of Jesus' teaching could be seen as making clear the distinction between a religion of observance and a transformation in which one is born from above, as he explains to Nicodemus, 'born of the Spirit' (Jn 3:8). Developing this thought, Schumacher says:

> Too often we communicate at the level of the word, and we don't change the world if we leave it there; unless the word, our message, our understanding, becomes incarnate, becomes flesh and dwells among us, nothing happens. This is a very deep insight of Christianity – that unless the word comes into the material world and becomes flesh, nothing happens.[17]

Conversion costs. Jesus chose a poor widow as a model of true religion. In giving two small coins to the Temple treasury she gives not out of her excess as many others do. Her donation is herself (Mk 12:44). To be true to oneself and to creation is costly. In Teilhard's account of the deep process of renewal overtaking him, in response to 'matter, throwing off its veil' to reveal 'its glorious unity', he finds he has become a stranger to his own, for he can now only be human 'on another plane'.[18] After Rachel Carson's revelation about the dire effects of chemical spraying, she was vilified by the offending companies as a 'woman with an overly sensitive nature, whose book was "more poisonous than the pesticides she condemns"' and dismissed as an alarmist, a romantic, a nature writer, a woman.[19] In 1988, Chico Mendes, a Brazilian, was murdered for his opposition to the destruction of his homeland. He came from a family of rubber trappers who made their living from the tropical forest. When the cattle ranchers and mining groups moved in to the area, they cut and burned the forest for grazing and short term benefit. Mendes' efforts to organise the rubber trappers against them led to fines, jail and at last to his death.

The new story of creation must issue for us in something equivalent to a renewal of our baptismal vows, where we re-commit ourselves to being truly immersed in the creative life flowing from Father, Son and Spirit. We have to be prepared to renounce our dependency on the empty promises of a con-sumerist lifestyle; to make of our faith something real and ac-tive, something to live and, if necessary, die for. Our word must become flesh. In *New Life for Old: On Desire and Becoming Human*, Vincent MacNamara notes that just as love of God is made man-ifest in love of neighbour so, too, private morality must address the demands of structural oppression. He quotes from Arch-bishop Rowan Williams who makes a similar point, namely, that mysticism and politics set the parameters for a fully Christian response. There is a political and ecological love which trans-lates and extends our love of neighbour.[20] As the extraordinary parable of the good Samaritan suggests, to be neighbour is to be someone who sees, saves, salves, picks up, accompanies, nour-ishes, attends. When we have set our Eucharistic table in the midst of creation, then the Spirit can make of us one body with all living beings, 'one spirit in Christ' (Eucharistic Prayer III).

Learning to listen to the cries of the Earth
The silence of a Eucharistic devotion needs to be fine-tuned. It is not narrowly a respectful silence 'before the Blessed Sacrament' but a deepening silence before the Word made flesh in creation. Beneath our human din, there are voices clamouring to be heard. Cries of the earth, cries of her children pushed to the edge of extinction, sighs of a great cosmic travail (Rom 8:22-3). The words of Isaiah in the mouth of the Servant of Yahweh are apt: 'Each morning he wakes me to hear, to listen like a disciple. The Lord Yahweh has opened my ear' (Is 50:4-5). As our hearing im-proves, we must question our unqualified support for a 'free-trade' which rolls over poor people and for multi-nationals

whose vested interests do not include a care for what is small and vulnerable. We are learning to beware of the bureaucrat, especially if he has a pen in his hand. For Dylan Thomas,

> the hand that signed the paper felled a city;
> five sovereign fingers taxed the breath,
> doubled the globe of dead and halved a country;
> these five kings did a king to death.[21]

We have mostly sided with the strong, the 'educated', the empire-builders. We call it progress but it is often window-dressing for national greed.

Remember the women of the Chipko ('tree huggers') movement in northern India in the early 1980s. From within their small communities they managed to save their trees and their living space from the logging companies. In a critique of the big international non-governmental organisations ('bingos') Panduran Hegde recalls what Sudesha Behen, the hill women of the Himalayas, say: 'It is the contribution of each household, a fistful of grain, that supports Chipko actions.' He continues:

> A fistful of grain might seem trivial – hardly an answer to the millions spent by international companies to 'uplift' the poor. But these Chipko women have brought greenery back to the barren hills of the Himalayas ... and regenerated biodiversity across thousands of hectares of forest.[22]

The image of 'a fistful of grain' is evocative within the Biblical tradition. It recalls the widow to whom Elijah is sent in a time of drought. She is about to prepare a last meal for herself and her son before she dies. Her reply to his request for 'a scrap of bread' is as follows: 'I have no baked bread, but only a handful of meal in a jar and a little oil in a jug.' Her generosity in preparing a scone for the prophet in such dire circumstances is rewarded with the promise of Yahweh: 'jar of meal shall not be spent, jug of oil shall not be emptied' until the rains come (1 Kings 17:11-16). Its resonance with the multiplication stories of Jesus cannot be missed. In Matthew (14:17-21), Jesus takes the five loaves and two fish, says the blessing, breaks the loaves and hands them to the disciples to distribute among the crowd; there are twelve baskets of scraps left over. This episode which is found in the synoptics and in John is kernel to his ministry. His action counters the hesitation of the disciples and their inclination to send the people away because there is not enough food. Like Jesus, the Chipko women seem to understand the power of 'a fistful of grain' given in hope. When the Eucharistic bread is shared in this spirit of 'joyful hope,' the whole creation is nourished.

Still the building goes on and the industrial noise drowns out the small whisper which we do not have ears to hear. They are the ears of the heart. When the woods have gone like the circus they will take the magic with them. Then we will listen in vain. In the National History Museum in Cape Town, the words of Walter Batiss (1948) reflecting on the cave paintings of South Africa are recorded.

> When I have been alone in a valley of Barkly East or high up in the Drakensberg of Natal, I have sensed the interpenetration of silences; one, the silence of the skies, and two, the valleys, and three, the mountains, four, the silence of the subsoils. And to these must be added a fifth silence: the mighty silence of all that is past; the angry footsteps of warlike men, the shrieks of young women in difficult childbirth, the sudden cries of injured children, moonlight songs of god worship, midnight noises of dances and sex play, laments of old women for their unreturned hunters; the whistle of the mountain rhebuck. The noise of a great activity has died and now only remains the silent paintings like lunar reflections of a great fiery sun that has set.

It is hard to believe that the word of God does not speak in these prophetic words, or that these words would not inspire a Eucharistic people.

An ecological conversion includes a call to contemplation
According to the document, *The Year of the Eucharist: Suggestions and Proposals,*
> We need to progress from the experience of liturgical silence … to the 'spirituality' of silence – to life's contemplative dimension. If not rooted in silence, the word can easily become dissipated, transformed into noise, or blunted.[23]

The call to an ecological conversion includes a call to contemplation; to gaze at nature from the inside, to look not only upwards to the mountain top but into the deep, to bring the whole of creation with its terror and beauty into view. Maura O'Halloran in her Buddhist monastery at Kannonji, north Japan, writes in her journal:

> I planted veggies, built a compost retainer, am preparing new beds. I feel such a peace puttering around in the dirt with all the wiggly, slimy, ugly little creatures. The creatures digging and fertilizing the garden are worth no more or less than I. I'm careful about them now; try not to disturb them, carry them to appropriate homes when they take over indoors.[24]

This is the kind of appreciative attitude towards life that an ecological conversion entails. It can be found in the lives of the early Irish saints. To take just one story out of hundreds: on the island of Iona, St Colmcille predicts the arrival of a heron, weary and exhausted from Ireland. He instructs the young monk to look out for the bird and, when it lands, to take heed to lift it tenderly and carry it to the house nearby. Having taken it in as a guest he will wait on it for three days and nights and feed it with anxious care.

Hospitality extends a welcome to all forms of life. What the monks found so absolutely in their encounter with the natural world was that God speaks in the plain chant of every creature. These stories come down to us as a blessing.

Even though I grew up along the seam where Crumlin met Walkinstown, my first memories are of my father digging in the garden, planting potatoes, cabbage, onions, beetroot, rhubarb, lettuce, etc.. We had gooseberries, blackcurrants, strawberries. There I met my first worms, snails, beetles, heard birdsong and put my hands into clay like the original potter. Children instinctively want to touch base, to make connections, to splash in puddles. The re-discovery of this instinct in ourselves will restore us to our place in that wider community. So, gather chestnuts, berries, plant a tree, a flower for we are gardeners at heart. This is not simple nostalgia, a prompt to romantic feelings for nature. Rather, it prepares us for deeper encounter. We are moved to something more than a wringing of hands at another oil spill or another polluted river.

For a faith community that insists so much on presence, we fail to deliver an adequate response until we attend to the quality of our own presence to the whole company of life. In the Book of Proverbs, wisdom is personified as one who shelters, feeds and invites the foolish to her table: 'come and eat my bread,/ drink the wine I have prepared!/ leave your folly and you will live,/ walk in the ways of perception' (Prov 9:5-6). It is an invitation to journey with awareness. The imagery is familiar to us, but we do not connect sufficiently Jesus who is our wisdom and Jesus as our bread of life. We eat and, filled with the Holy Spirit, we learn how to live, how to be present. Without presence we do not notice the beauty and terror of the world; we don't experience it deliberately as colour, taste, sound, smell, touch. Without presence, we do not come into the real presence of other creatures and know ourselves addressed by them. We do not find the energy to save.

The practice of attention

Our thinking mind can busy itself endlessly skimming the surface like the Pond Skater *Gerris lacustris*, (but without the insect's intelligence and amazing abilities), and fail to appreciate that there is a sacredness that cannot be understood by thought. It can only be approached through presence. Eckhart Tolle remarks:

> When you bring your attention to a stone, a tree or an animal, you can sense how still it is, and in doing so the same stillness arises within you. You sense how deeply it rests in Being – completely at one with what it is and where it is. In realizing this, you too come to a place of rest deep within yourself. On the other hand, through your recognition and awareness, nature comes to know itself for it has been waiting for you, as it were, for millions of years.[25]

We are one with each other; made for each other. It is not surprising that our spiritual health is threatened by our increasing separation from a direct experience of the natural world. The scriptural text applied to the marriage bond could as easily be applied to our bond with nature: 'What God has joined together, we must not separate.'

To participate in the Eucharist is to be drawn into the web of interconnected life through the presence of the risen Christ. In our communion with him in the sacramental bread and wine we are woken into that stillness enveloping all being. The injunction to 'stay awake' corresponds to waiting in attention for the Master's return. Tolle reads Jesus' account of the Five Wise Virgins (as opposed to the foolish ones) who keep a good supply of oil in readiness for the Bridegroom's arrival as a parable about living in awareness, living in the power of the Now.[26] For him, silence leads to presence and, in Eucharistic terms, a silence of 'amazement' flows from Christ's presence to all creation.

Yet, we so often live outside amazement. Chatter oppresses silence. Celebrity, fashion, the body beautiful merely distract from the sacred heart of every being. Pornography denies the real presence of the human body. It displaces the erotic which celebrates sexuality by offering a distorted version of reality, omitting relationship, mystery, individuality, fun. The Eucharistic body of Jesus counters such displacement. It takes us deeper into ourselves, calls us, as the body of Christ, into communion with every living being. Celebrating Eucharist then becomes the means by which we effect an ecological conversion. It is not only about separating our refuse, or cutting down on journeys by car, laudable though these are. Tolle puts it starkly:

> Are you polluting the world or cleaning up the mess? You are responsible for your inner space; nobody else is, just as you are responsible for the planet. As within, so without: If humans clear inner pollution, then they will also cease to create outer pollution.[27]

In Eucharistic Prayer III, when we ask that the Spirit 'fill us', we are asking to be filled with the Spirit-breath, to be enlivened in our breathing and to be connected to all that is. How we live matters! Our practice of being present is not simply an interior posture. Rather, it issues in activity, however small and apparently insignificant. Our response might be no more than the regular drop of water we share with a pot plant. Joining a nature group. Supporting farmers' markets. Taking the children to the woods; being led by their sense of wonder. Going on a field trip. Listening to people who are captivated by aspects of the wild.

Eucharistic encounter with the Lord of creation sends us back to planet Earth. At its heart is the Eucharistic Prayer which, far from offering us an escape from earthly reality, involves us in a process of transformation. The future to which we look forward is not happening 'out there' but is experienced as already present – the eschatological tension between 'already' and 'not yet'. We can live that future along the path of awareness, welcoming the risen Lord who comes as surely as 'the dawn from on high' (Lk 1:78). Given that the universe has become aware of itself in our species, we keep our lamps lit on behalf of all.

The Eucharist is a sacrament for the whole of creation
In a Christian context, one thinks of the seed falling where there is no depth of soil. The plant springs up but cannot sustain. Nevertheless, one continues to plant. The Apostolic Letter of John Paul II, (*MND* par 24), takes account of this consideration. He notes how St Paul 'closely relates meal and proclamation', so that the dismissal at the end of the Eucharist charges the congregation to body forth what they have celebrated. This they can only do when they have assimilated 'through personal and communal meditation the *values* which the Eucharist expresses, the *attitudes* it inspires, the *resolutions* to which it gives rise' (italics mine), (MND par 25). A Eucharistic ethic/spirituality embedded in creation will attempt to embody in local practice the principles of all life – diversity, subjectivity (where 'those of low degree are exalted' (Lk 1:52),) and communion. The Pastoral Letter from the Archbishop of Cashel and Emly (Ireland), in 2003, is one such example of promoting a new awareness, especially in regard to our use of water.[28] It asks us to critique our environmental commissions and omissions as 'ecological sin', as truly offences against the Earth. In other words, it calls for planetary modesty, for the kind of humility described so wonderfully by Dag Hammarskjold:

> To have humility is to experience reality, not in relation to ourselves but in its sacred independence. It is to see, judge, and act from the point of rest in ourselves. Then, how much disappears, and all that remains falls into place. In the point of rest at the centre of our being, we encounter a world where all things are at rest in the same way. Then a tree becomes a

mystery, a cloud, a revelation, each man a cosmos of whose riches we can only catch glimpses. The life of simplicity is simple, but it opens to us a book in which we never get beyond the first syllable.[29]

And to rest at the centre is the goal of Eucharist. It is there that one finds one's centre. The Eucharistic community is not just to be 'a "sacrament" for humanity' (*EE*, par 22), but a sacrament for the whole of creation. By being in communion with Christ, the human community is filled with the Holy Spirit and comes to rest within creation itself. (Observance of the Sabbath in the book of Deuteronomy (5:14) specifies rest for all, including ox, donkey or any of the animals!) With a little thought, Sunday could become a day given to the outdoors. Having made communion and joined in the chorus of acclaim of all creation, it would be good to renew the habit of visiting neighbours, including those not of our species. To meet new friends, to learn the names of living beings who don't have an email address. This is quite a different order of being than that one sensed by Thomas Berry who notices in Western industrial society a hidden rage against life itself and against the restraints of our earthly condition.[30]

The truth of Christian conversion issues in the resolution to live in a new way. The understanding that supports a change of heart towards the created world is enhanced by turning towards the wonders that science has unveiled for us. This is not to uncritically accept the role of science in human meaning but to couple it with religious insight. As Albert Einstein put it: 'Science without religion is lame, religion without science is blind.'[31] Edward O. Wilson's description of the small group of scientists specialising in the classification of new life 'from bacteria to fungi to insects' and 'inundated with new species almost to the breaking point', points to a human community that befriends life.[32] Is there a similar earnestness and urgency to be found in people of faith? We can only hope that Wilson's cautious optimism regarding the growing prominence of the environment in religious thought is justified, as he imagines the approach of, firstly, the saints and radical theologians, then growing numbers of the faithful and then, warily, bishops, patriarchs, and imams.

The recovery of lost connections between faith and science honours the Christ who came so that 'they may have life and have it abundantly,' and not only the human species. (Jn 10:10). In the words of the prophet: 'And what does the Lord require of you but to do justice, and to love kindness, and to walk humbly with your God' (Mic 6:8), and this in the context of all creation.

CHAPTER FOUR

Celebrating Eucharist in a Holy Communion

We can no more live singly than light can fall on one place only.
Peter Sirr[1]

The question remains: what happens in practice? How can a Christian community be helped to experience the creation dimension of its worship? How can it be moved towards an ecological conversion, towards understanding that the Eucharist is always celebrated on the altar of the world, that every liturgy is a cosmic liturgy? One might demur: are the other aspects, the Eucharist as sacrifice, as memorial, as thanksgiving, not equally in need of attention? Of course all aspects are interlaid with each other; they do not stand alone as false alternatives. My attention, however, sharpened by multiple threats to the community of all life and to the fabric of our dwelling, has focused on how the transformation of the Universe is heralded in the presence of bread and wine at the Eucharistic event. Our joyful expectation of Christ's return is shared by the whole creation as together we give praise for the first fruits of that fulfilment. Such is the reach and grandeur of the Eucharist where everything is drawn into a holy communion.

In this short chapter, I will briefly refer to particular Eucharistic moments and texts and draw attention to their cosmic significance. As indicated earlier, it is a question of evocation more than addition. Much is already in place but needs to be highlighted. I merely make some suggestions which are far from comprehensive.

I have already alluded to the recognition from earliest times of the rising sun as a point of reference for our worship. The loss of this sense of direction (orientation) in our prayer and liturgy is more than sentimental. It speaks of our disconnection from the source of life and the dwarfing of our ambition to simply human concerns. In the past, we consciously buried our dead facing east so that they might face the rising sun and be ready to greet their Lord whose loving kindness comes to us 'like the dawn from on high' (Lk 1:78). At the winter solstice, the darkest time of the year, a dawn Mass in which we deliberately turn our attention eastwards would make for a memorable celebration. In this way we would also find ourselves in solidarity with those waiting in the Newgrange chamber for the sun to rise. A little imagination is called for and a deepening appreciation of what is meant by the phrase, 'the risen Christ'. It's time to re-educate ourselves to the wider frame of reference to which we belong.

But the wider frame becomes home to us in a particular place, our parish. Older festivals incorporated walking the parish boundary, not so much as territorial enforcement but as a reminder of where this community lives. The tradition of rogation days, now fallen into disuse, upheld these connections in the ritual of blessing the land and its produce. This instinct is all but lost on us, the affinity or closeness to the land of our own place, the wisdom of the soil, its contours. The Eucharist is celebrated on the altar of the world but, specifically, on *this* patch of earth. In response, we can acknowledge the ground that sustains us by supporting local markets and encouraging what builds community not only with ourselves but with the local flora and fauna. This kind of saving activity must enter our celebration. This is not to reduce it to a narrow community perspective but to understand the universal in the local, the local in the universal.

Worth re-visiting is the Eucharistic fast. It could benefit from a good catechesis. Its symbolic force goes beyond words. At one level, it draws attention to the Bread of Life and our sharing in the fruits of the earth; at another, it is a reaching out to those who are hungry; at another, it marks our journey to church in awareness of a world of broken human realities and ecological destruction.

The rich symbolism of the holy water font at the entrance is sometimes overlooked. To bless myself with the gift of water from the font is a recall to baptismal waters and the mythological journey from death to life. It is also to dip my fingers into the mystery of planet Earth, the water planet. It alerts us to what is involved in crossing a threshold. Illuminating in this context is Ezekiel's vision of the life-giving water flowing from below the Temple refreshing all creation (47:1-12).

In a functional age, we need these rituals more than ever. They speak to a depth in us. Similarly, our traditional music, where used in liturgy, is felt in the marrowbone. Seamus Heaney writes of the 'given note' of *Port na bPúcaí*, the elemental 'spirit music' of air and wave entering our bloodstream – 'bits of a tune/ Coming in on loud weather/ Though nothing like melody.'[2] Uileann pipes, fiddle, whistle and harp seem peculiarly fitted to nudge us towards a celebration within our own region. They can live quite comfortably with organ music.

And what of language? The language we use needs minding. Religious language is the language of mystic and lover. Dogmatic formulae have their place but do not touch the heart. In George Herbert the priest and poet agree: 'A verse may find him who a sermon flies/ and turn delight into a sacrifice.'[3] We have a dual tradition in Ireland. We should dare to use the Irish language in our liturgy even when neither priest nor congregation is particularly fluent. Our failure to do so may seem insignificant. But to recall that fifty percent of the remaining six thousand languages of human-speak will die out in the next century invites the question: will Irish be one of them? At its best, every language is an expression of the human spirit as it encounters mysterious reality. One language cannot be simply replaced by another. There is a soul-loss when a language dies. When we pray in Irish, though the inflection may not be quite familiar to us, we are claiming our inheritance in solidarity with those who have gone before us. *Guímís chun an Athair.*

Where the Christian story converged with that older Druidic tradition of wells and trees and seasonal wisdom, how eloquent it became. In that exchange, the celebration of Imbolg at the beginning of the lambing season, for instance, crystallised into the figure of Brigid who stands in the doorway of spring. The seasonal festivals – midwinter, spring, midsummer, first harvest – flowered in a new calendar celebrating Christ's birth, Easter, the feasts of St John and St Martin. The festival at harvest-time where both ends of the year met, so to speak, easily accommodated that otherworldly dimension evoked by All Souls and All

Saints. At this hour of disconnection from the natural world, perhaps our festivals need to revisit their earthly roots. These great feasts can provide opportunities for making plain the dove-tailing of Eucharist and creation. The inclusion of a Season of Creation to stand alongside Lent, Easter, Advent and Christmas in the liturgical year would be a welcome development. It is proposed that such a season might fall each year on the four or five Sundays preceding the feast of St Francis of Assisi (4 October). The driving force behind this initiative is the Lutheran theologian, Norman Habel, (www.seasonofcreation .com),who has already prepared a three year cycle of suitable liturgies. These could be easily adapted to take account of particular theological nuance.

Where it is possible to celebrate the Eucharist out of doors, at mid-summer, for example, connections are more easily made. Our voices can blend with those of animal, insect and, if we are lucky, some foreign visitors, swallow, chiff-chaff, corncrake, cuckoo. A Corpus Christi procession in natural surroundings can be an opportunity to rejoice with the living world. When I have had the opportunity to celebrate the Eucharist on a Mass rock in the Slieve Blooms for a group of young people, my awareness was of being brought down to size. In this wild landscape we were offering our worship without the cosiness of artificial light and heat and an amplified voice. We were unprotected from the elements just like the parishioners 'attending Mass' in a roofless Ballintubber Abbey during much of its history. Remnants of faith are lodged in such places. These lines of mine suggest the ongoing revelatory moment to be experienced there:

Pilgrimage
We travelled up the Barrow stream
and traced it to its source;
in a silent glen
we found a holy well.

Lost in that mountain fold
we found our way again –
the heavens wide,
the landscape prayer.

A similar insight is to be found in psalm 148 where sun, moon and stars are encouraged to join in praise of God together with all creation – orchards, forests, wild and domestic animals, snakes and birds, men and women, young and old. This universal gathering, according to the John Paul II, 'brings us into a sort of cosmic church', the aisles of which are filled with the regional choirs of God's creatures while the heavens form the overarching apse.[4]

A liturgical art that incorporates these insights is more necessary than ever. The relationship between cross and cosmos is variously represented by incising the cross on the globe or painting the globe on the cross. The Tree of Life motif seeks to express a similar interweaving of Christ and creation. This religious instinct has a long history. We find it on the island of Iona on two crosses dating from the ninth century which combine natural and scriptural elements. Francis of Assisi's creative understanding of the Bethlehem scene, where the animals must play their part, can still instruct. Should animals threatened with extinction not accompany, (or temporarily replace), the ox and ass? What about a cosmic crib with unfamiliar animals coming to worship? Easter gardens in churches offer similar opportunities for celebrating biodiversity and taking stock of our losses. Much can be done. When we express in mixed media the communion of all beings with the Father we acknowledge our common worship 'in spirit and truth' (Jn 4:23).

Evoking the cosmic dimension
In the Eucharist we begin with the Sign of the Cross, sign of Trinitarian love and of protection. The wonderful Lorica prayer attributed to St Patrick moves in the background. 'I arise today', invoking the Trinity in the strength of heaven and in the firmness of earth. *The Deer's Cry* of Patrick's breastplate weaves a cosmic-Christian spell: 'Christ behind me, Christ before me, Christ on my right, Christ on my left …'

The Penitential Rite can invite us to an ecological conversion, to reflect on our relationship with the Earth. Our salvation story in Eucharistic Prayer IV recalls the breach of trust in regard to our twin responsibilities from the beginning, to serve the creator and 'to rule over' all creatures. Mindless pollution, careless attitudes towards the rights of other species, the creation of excessive waste through excessive consumption, call for new eyes and ears. For when we sin against the earth, we sin against ourselves and sin against succeeding generations of children. When spoken from within the community of all living beings, the words, 'I confess to Almighty God and to you my brothers and sisters,' find a new register. It's a beguiling concept to imagine other species (our brothers and sisters) praying with Blessed Mary, angels and saints to the Lord of creation on our behalf.

The Gloria speaks in lofty formulaic language: 'You are the holy one, you are the Lord, You alone are the Most High, Jesus Christ with the Holy Spirit, in the glory of God the Father.' But Jesus is also the eminently Human One. A Gloria from the ground up, would give some body to this Trinitarian acclaim:

Glory to you, Father of all, for bringing us to birth and for the thousand ways you speak to us of yourself in every creature.

Glory to you, Jesus our Lord, for sharing our life and inviting us to come from the byroads of unawareness to the table of unconditional love.

Glory to you, creative Spirit. We feel your pulse in the wind and in fire. Together with the Father and Son, you refresh and renew our whole being and lead us into communion with all creation.

Glory and praise to you, Father, Son and Holy Spirit.

When we read the scriptural texts from an ecological perspective they speak powerfully to us of urgent realities we need to hear. The homilist with a feeling for the earth can prompt this kind of listening. The maternal image that Jesus applies to himself, for example, of a hen gathering her chicks around her at a time of danger, is instructive in a time of alarming climate change. A contemporary reading of the parable of the talents can rouse us to our responsibilities for nurturing and protecting the earth-gifts which have been entrusted to us. The Word of God is both challenge and consolation. Needless to say that supplementary readings of prophetic force should not be thought unworthy of our consideration. What needs to inform our attendance at the table of the Word, however, is not the latest threat to our well-being but a conversion to a new way of being in the world.

The concerns addressed in the Creed are those of the Council of Nicea and not immediately relevant to us. When my fourteen year old nephew turned to his mother at a Sunday Mass to ask, 'What does "begotten not made" mean?' he was genuinely curious. Religious language can be problematic. On the other hand, within the traditional formula of the Creed, there is the basis of a creation spirituality. The intimate relationship of the Trinity with creation is expressed through the Father, creator 'of all that is, seen and unseen;' through Jesus Christ 'through whom all things were made' and through the Holy Spirit, 'the Lord and giver of life'. When my experience of creation opens up to the mystery of Trinitarian love, I can be moved to say, 'I believe.' In our caring for the earth our faith-words become flesh.

The Prayers of the Faithful should always include prayer for the living Earth to which we belong, a reminder that the Earth is not a commodity that belongs to us. 'When we see land as a community to which we belong, we may begin to use it with love and respect.'[5] This is also an opportunity to direct the praying heart to the local community of all beings, 'seen and unseen,' some of whom only reveal themselves to our eyes under a microscope. May our prayer rise like pollen and disperse where it will. Such awareness anticipates our offering of bread and wine, the fruits of the earth.

The Presentation of the Gifts from within the community is not meant to be simply their transfer from one place to another. The ritual is important. This is the daily bread we pray for, bread for today's Eucharist. It represents the 'work of human hands' and what 'the earth has given' through the work of the many tiny creatures who make our soil capable of producing food. (It would be small-minded of us to exclude their offering.) There is, according to Pope Benedict, a 'synergy of forces' at work to bring bread to the table; from the living soil to the gift of sunshine and rain; from the one who plants to the one who harvests the wheat; from the mill to the oven.[6] Our presentation of 'gifts' continues the faith tradition of offering the fruits of the earth as Abel, Abraham and Melchisedech did, the acceptance of which brings peace and salvation to the world (Eucharistic Prayer I and IV).

In the liturgies of the Greek Orthodox Church, this 'lifting up' of the gifts is referred to as the *Anaphora*. It is a more deliberate and impressive ceremony than is found in the Roman rite. According to John Zizioulas, eminent theologian and Metropolitan of Pergamon, 'This action, whereby humanity gives thanks and offers the gifts of creation to God, is of equal importance to God's act of sending the Holy Spirit to transform the gifts into the body and blood of Christ.'[7] He describes the human role within creation in ministerial terms; we are celebrants, 'priests of creation,' a role which does not replace but elevates creation's ongoing relationship with God! In his liturgical vision, every person participates in the priestly task of 'offering', understood less as sacrifice than as a bringing into communion, which extends beyond the ritual action to the whole of life. It involves:

> relating to creation in such a respectful way that the uniqueness of each entity and the interconnectedness of everything are so recognised and honoured that nature is enabled to develop its full potential as a 'bearer of life'.[8]

When Vatican II described the People of God as sharing in Christ's priesthood it was opening up the possibility of a new relationship with creation. According to the relevant document, *Lumen Gentium*, 'the believer must learn to recognise the inner nature of creation, its value and orientation to the praise of God.'[9] This kind of understanding suggests that in the symbolic action of offering bread and wine we are making a profound ecological gesture. A truly loving relationship with creation is expressed as together we are drawn into God's life of communion.

The story of Nikolai Vavilov is salutary for those of us who pick up our bread, without much thought, from bakery or supermarket. Born in 1837, he worked at the All Union Institute of Applied Botany in St Petersburg. In the 1920s and 30s, he collected and classified tens of thousands of crop species – his wheat collection alone included 26,000 varieties. On false charges made against him by the geneticist Lysenko, he was banished to Siberia and died there. But the story continues. In 1942 the Germans besieged St Petersburg (Leningrad) and cut off the food supply. Over half a million people died. At the

Institute, however, hungry scientists remained to protect the vast collection of seeds from rats and the elements. Fourteen died of starvation surrounded by bags of rare seeds which they could have eaten to save their lives. Their costly gesture towards future generations should not be forgotten in the breaking of bread.[10] Seed and sacrifice are drawn together in these Eucharistic words: 'Unless a grain of wheat falls on the ground and dies, it remains a single grain; but if it dies, it yields a rich harvest' (Jn 12:24).

Reflecting on this text in his homily for the Feast of Corpus Christi (2006), Pope Benedict explains:

> The mystery of the Passion is hidden in the bread made of ground grain. Flour, the ground wheat, presupposes the death and resurrection of the grain. In being ground and baked, it carries in itself once again the same mystery of the Passion. Only through death does resurrection arrive as fruit and new life.[11]

The Preface, the first part of the Eucharistic Prayer, invites us to a cosmic celebration – 'The joy of the resurrection renews the whole world' (Easter season). It is addressed to the Father, 'the source of life and goodness', to whom we give thanks through Christ our Lord. The unceasing nature of this acclaim is especially evident in creation and is caught up now in our worship: 'All creation rightly gives you praise.' It is worth repeating that the presence of creation in the Eucharist is not dependent on our yea or nay. It is there inasmuch as we are there, its acclaim preceding ours by billions of years. In the Eucharist, no division is recognised, no discrimination. In the Sanctus, we join with angels and saints and with every creature as we acknowledge how heaven and earth are full of God's glory. Our polyphonic melody harmonises with the great liturgy of angel song.

The Eucharistic Prayer is the core and forms the real 'action' of the Eucharist. It is uniquely God's graceful initiative, taking place through human speech, for which all creation is in expectation. In the Eucharistic Prayer, Father, Son and Spirit make themselves accessible to us through the fruits of the earth and announce a new creation. In this way, we are caught up in the drama of Trinitarian love in which the universal principles of community, diversity and interiority mingle and find personal expression.

This outpouring of Trinitarian love shapes the Eucharistic Prayer. We move from praise of the Father 'who so loved the world that he sent his only Son,' to commemoration of Jesus' self-giving: 'this is my body which will be given up for you … my blood (which) will be shed for you.' Then from our offering of 'the life-giving bread (and) saving cup' to our petitions that the Spirit make fruitful this Eucharist. This is the consummate Christian prayer that cannot be reduced to our own size. It takes up all time from the rising of the sun to its setting. It crosses the bounds that commonly divide the living from the dead. It opens itself up to the billions of years of evolution and does not lose count of lost generations of ancestors and of species which are extinct.

In its expression of praise, and by the power of the Spirit over the gifts, the whole creation is transformed into Christ. This 'irradiation' of Christ's presence, like a pebble thrown into a lake, ripples out to the furthest edge of our expanding universe. How wonderful to think of the universe seeded with Christ's promise of fulfilment and how one day we shall sing (from the same hymn sheet) with every creature in the heavenly kingdom (Eucharistic Prayer IV). It would be presumptuous to imagine that the created world is oblivious to the great event of Christ's death and resurrection at the heart of the Eucharist. Indeed, Pope Benedict points out that 'This little piece of white Host, this bread of the poor, appears to us as a synthesis of creation.' Furthermore, with a nod towards Teilhard de Chardin, he adds: 'We can detect in the piece of bread' that creation aspires to and is 'projected towards divinisation, towards the holy wedding feast, towards union with the Creator.'[12] The fruits of the earth are speaking of Christ! We can go further. By partaking of the sacred Host we are drawn into communion not just with Christ and with one another but with all creation.

In the gesture of raising the consecrated bread and wine to the great Trinitarian acclaim, 'through him, with him, in him,' the answering Amen, (echoing the Holy, Holy, Holy), is an affirmation shared by the whole creation. It really calls out to be sung and to be answered with jubilation. The Eucharist which is given to us is no local matter. It is Love poured out for us over all the Earth. Our muted responses fail to make that clear.

The Our Father involves the universe in its longing: 'thy kingdom come, thy will be done,' and in its petitions 'give us this day our daily bread' and 'deliver us from evil'. When we say 'Our Father', the whole cosmos is praying through us to the Source of life and expressing its hope of fulfilment. It recalls Mary's Magnificat which looks forward to a time when 'the proud-hearted' will be scattered, the starving filled, the disregarded ones raised up. The celebrant can easily include this cosmic dimension in the introduction. He might say: 'Jesus taught us to call God our Father and so we have the courage to say *with all creation* ...

The anxiety of 'Deliver us, Lord, from every evil' is a shared anxiety of a troubled and suffocating Earth. We need to be delivered from evils of our own making; the onslaught on our living space; the attack on the life systems that sustain us; from our slavery to consumption; from our horizontal lives. In the ritual of the Sign of Peace our peace-making must be inclusive of every being, our blessing of *shalom* alight particularly on the flora and fauna of our own region. At times, it will be opportune to name certain threatened environments or individual species and to open our hearts to them. Peace is exchanged when we address another being as you, as thou. It is a gesture of positive discrimination against the down-sizing of life itself to an 'it'.

Again, when the celebrant raises the host with the words, 'This is the Lamb of God, happy are those who are called to his supper,' creation bows down in worship. The supper mentioned is the 'marriage supper of the Lamb,' to which the whole of creation is invited (Rev 19:7). Through our sacramental communion, we are filled with the fire of the Spirit who renews the face of the earth. The 'spiritual communion' of creation with Christ should not be disregarded as a poor imitation of the actual reception of Christ's body and blood. The 'eager longing' of creation hints at a worship 'in spirit and in truth,' (Jn 4:24). Similarly, an over-emphasis on a private Eucharistic spirituality fails to recognise the cosmic significance of Christ's self-giving for all.

The dismissal, 'The Mass is ended, go in peace,' sends us out to be neighbour to all, for we have glimpsed how we might live on the earth with one another as a new creation – suffering when the other suffers, being joyful in the other's joy. We go out to welcome biodiversity, to learn to live a Trinitarian love. Eucharist takes us through the Paschal drama to the realisation that, in the words of Peter Sirr, 'We can no more live singly than light can fall on one place only.'

The dismissal calls us also to a vision of beauty, calls us to live in harmony, peace and justice with all beings. This sounds familiar. It is precisely what it means to be living in the kingdom of God. It is the same reality to which the Navajo Indians commit themselves in their daily recitation – a prayer which echoes the prayer attributed to St Patrick, 'Christ beside me, Christ before me, Christ at my right, Christ at my left.'

In beauty may I walk
In beauty may I walk
All day long may I walk
Through the returning seasons may I walk
On the trail marked with pollen may I walk
With grasshoppers about my feet may I walk
With dew about my feet may I walk
With beauty may I walk
With beauty behind me may I walk
With beauty above me may I walk
With beauty below me may I walk
With beauty all around me may I walk
In old age, wandering on a trail of beauty, lively may I walk
In old age, wandering on a trail of beauty, living again may I walk
It is finished in beauty
It is finished in beauty.

For the Navajo, beauty, *hozho*, is more than the achievement of art and craft; it refers to a total environment of all that is positive in life. To live (and die) in beauty is to be incorporated into the beauty of the universe.[13] But the world which the Navajo long for has to be created every day. Christians envisage that world in the Eucharist when they recall what Jesus did, how he took the bread in his hands, and having blessed it, he broke it and gave it to his disciples saying, 'Take this, this is my body.' We are called to live in appreciation of the gifts of life, to live in thanksgiving, to commit ourselves in practice to the wholeness and holiness of our being here. How else can we worship the God who loves the world so much that he sent us a Jesus on fire with the Holy Spirit? Only a Eucharistic spirituality which recognises the presence of Trinitarian love in the imperilled creation with its countless poor is worthy of us. There is much to do.

CONCLUSION

A community of hope on behalf of all creation

The goal of this reflection has been to uphold a creation context as essential to an integral celebration of the Eucharist. For its cosmic dimension to be realised, it is necessary to embrace the story of the universe as our own sacred story. And not simply at an intellectual level but in terms of our whole being. In this respect, conversion (for individual and community) is paramount. The New Story is fascinating, but to allow it to remain disconnected from our faith-filled response to the Creator, even as we offer the fruits of the earth, does seem a serious omission. In essence, the call to conversion means not only coming to terms with the profound meaning of Eucharist as 'the washing of the feet' of the poorest, but of extending that gesture to every living being, especially those species under threat from mindless human activity. Graced with this insight, the Christian assembly then becomes a community of hope on behalf of all creation.

At the Campbell Seminar held at Columbia Theological Seminary (2001), the participants identified 'despair' as the prevailing mood of humankind, creating a vacuum that is filled with the failed rhetoric of 'the world's possessing peoples' who seem incapable of either self-knowledge or planetary responsibility.[1] This 'despair' is not the opposite of hope but arises from a flawed optimism. ('The official optimism' of the ideologies consider any questioning of their outlook to be a sin against the spirit of the age.) Perhaps, hope is closer to joy. Derek Walcott describes joy, as 'the bright opposite of nothing (which) ... descends on the unexpecting heart in the midst of the worst suffering ... because it knows that the world is stupendous and that we are privileged to be in it.'[2] Christian hope, like joy, is a gift of love freely given in the figure of Jesus Christ in whom God's love encounters us in person; a gift made present, par excellence, in the Eucharist. It is a hope 'against' all the false hopes of those who do not reckon with the reality of a limited biosphere and a shared existence. Hope is not merely a longing for the 'next' world as an escape, but is a priceless gift to bring us to our senses in this one.

Our resurrection hope, centred on God's abiding presence to us in the Eucharist, commits us to care, as participants, for all creation. In the language of Jesus, we are called to wake up, to open our eyes to what is happening to us, to our earth and its inhabitants, to the poor and endangered. Not simply to hear the challenging Word but to put it into practice. For hope is made manifest in our response to particular situations. One community will build Newgrange, another will stand by their trees, yet another will devise a Biodiversity Action Strategy for their area. One particularly hope-filled response is the ecumenical initiative of the major Christian Churches in Britain and Ireland. Its name, *Operation Noah*, recalling the Rainbow Covenant of Genesis (6:17-22), is well chosen for a time of peril. Launched in October 2004 in Coventry, its hope is to curb our human-induced contribution to global warming. It asks that we enter into a personal covenant with the Lord of creation to stop harming the planet and its creatures by the irresponsible way we live. The Eucharistic covenant which Christ makes with us demands a response. Is there a better one than a commitment to the living Earth, home to our brothers and sisters of all species? It's time to wake up. Time to jump aboard and make ourselves heard.

The worst effects of climate change won't make distinction between Moslem, Catholic or Jew. What is important is that we link up with one another. Internet, for instance, boasts a huge number of websites committed to caring for the Earth, with names like 'The Web of Hope', 'Climate Care', 'The Gaia Foundation', 'Friends of the Earth', 'Common Ground' and, more ominously, 'Climate Crisis'. It's time to enlist.

Hope for our home-place, however, cannot be separated from hope for the poor, that most threatened section of humanity. Bill Rees, a population ecologist at the University of British Columbia, has famously pointed out that we would need four or five more Earths right now to bring everyone on the planet to the same level of consumption and well-being as the average Canadian. We live in a world where between 800 and 840 million people in developing countries face chronic malnutrition; around 200 million children under age five suffer from acute and chronic protein and energy deficiencies; 40,000 people die each day as a consequence of hunger and malnutrition.[3] Every celebration of the Eucharist must remember those who are hungry as it remembers Christ, the Bread of Life. Drawing on the traditional image of a sanctuary lamp to describe the manner by which the poor witness, (as Jesus did), to God's presence in the world, Leonardo Boff writes:

> It is often they who keep the divine light, the light of the sacred and of the Mystery behind human existence, burning as if in a sanctuary. It is they who ensure that the most decisive element in history is not weakened or lost.[4]

We celebrate Eucharist to embody hope
Against this background of injustice, and with the knowledge of the increasing threat to our planet and its myriad species, we celebrate Eucharist to embody hope. We are not celebrating alone. To claim otherwise would distort our own being and effectively silence the rest of creation. For we are not apart from the earth but its unique achievement. This is our great challenge: to find our place among the others as the one thing necessary for healing and survival. To lose our soul, according to Jesus, is accounted our greatest loss, and greater still when we include in our self-definition, the soulfulness of earth. We are covenanted to each other. As spouse, the created world addresses us in hope. We are called to be in communion, to uphold difference, to refine our ability to speak and to listen with our whole body. Teilhard advances a similar intuition when he prays: 'Over every living thing which is to spring up, to grow, to flower, to ripen during this day say again the words: This is my Body.'[5] This is the kind of understanding of Eucharist that generates hope for all creation. But hope is offered us as a task as well as a gift. We are to live as if the gift were already ours and within reach. 'The kingdom of heaven is close to you.' From this perspective, implications follow. (The following might be considered a contemporary formulation of the four 'cardinal' virtues,

rendered inadequately in English as prudence, justice, temperance and fortitude, with pride of place given to *prudentia*, that 'clear-eyed, magnanimous recognition of reality'[6].)

Firstly, the practice of emptying our cupboard, of learning the meaning of enough; of making our way with greater trust in Providence and respect for the earth than in a growing pension fund. It is not simply about asceticism. It is the desire, rather, to live with a simple elegance. The Japanese have a word *wabi-sabi* to describe a philosophy of sufficiency and restraint such as you find in their Tea Ceremony with its ritualised gravity.[7] It translates easily into a Eucharistic way of life where the humble, down-to-earth realities are valued above what is large and expensive. Bread and wine are never just base materials. The grain in old wood or the sound of rain rinsing the trees triggers joy. In rejecting the consumerist imperative, we are doing so in view of Jesus' self-emptying on the cross as his final expression of hope in God's promises.

Secondly, there is the Eucharistic practice of siding with the excluded, of standing with the women on a ubiquitous Golgotha, of showing our hand on their behalf when it comes to fellow creatures of all species threatened with extinction. In this way we are recalling the table-fellowship Jesus consistently makes with outcasts, the 'prostitutes and sinners'. Despite the personal cost, he reaches out to a leper, thereby making himself 'unclean' so that he can no longer openly enter a town, his 'secret' like a frailty exposed (Mk 1:45). From the very beginning, collections of money were taken up for the poor at the community assemblies, a practice to which St Paul applies the term 'liturgy' (Rom 15:27; 2 Cor 9:12 f). The bottom line, it appears, is that 'we cannot share the Eucharistic bread while refusing to share our daily bread.'[8]

Thirdly, is the practice of upholding the goodness of the living Earth and the interiority of all species. By doing so, we are recognising that creation awaits our approval as a child awaits the attention of a loving parent. Not only are we asked to respond to the splendour of the Earth but to the fact that the universe awakens to its own beauty through us. (Of course, in a most important sense, the Earth as a parent also nurtures us into the people we are.) When we begin to grasp the scope of this responsibility, we are moved to act. We might, for instance, decide to take a stand against the refusal of many corporations to include the real costs to livelihoods and habitats in reckoning economic growth. Where the only value worth considering becomes the economic one, then communion, diversity and the unique voice of every living thing is set aside. Nature is objectified and our inheritance sold off. By taking up the cause of the living community in our Eucharistic celebration, we are anticipating the joy of sharing with all creation in the Father's house.

Lastly, in searching out creative alternatives about what it means to be human, we are responding to a diminution of spirit in western society with our growing disconnection from nature. We need to be made whole again, to re-invent ourselves *within the new cosmic story* through play and ceremony and a shared vision of life.[9] To do so, we must be open to those sources of wisdom which speak of our intimacy with the natural world. These are to be found particularly in the wisdom of indigenous peoples, in the experience of women whose contribution to political discourse has traditionally been undervalued, in the classical religious traditions and in the discoveries of modern science. Above all, we need to embrace the Eucharist as our hope-filled encounter with Jesus who through his blood makes communion a present reality between men and women, rich and poor, human and non-human. For John Zizioulas, the Eucharist is that privileged place of encounter with God and creation where 'what is enacted symbolically so forms a person's vision of reality that this spills over into how that person acts in the world'.[10] As liturgical beings, celebrants of creation, we are involved in a saving activity that goes deeper than a simple pragmatic or ethical response to the ecological crisis; we are drawn into a communion of life-giving love within creation.

Maybe nothing seems to happen. Perhaps, it's only a butterfly's laboured flapping. Nevertheless, the moment of fulfilment is sensed as here but tantalisingly out of reach, sensed as the first shoots of a new creation. For in the very act of celebrating Eucharist we recognise that the bread broken – Christ's body – is meant as a healing gesture for all. And that if we can allow this new understanding to take hold of us, to 'requisition' us, (*aggareuein*), press us into service like a Simon of Cyrene on behalf of every threatened creature, then the 'radiance' of the Eucharist must shine forth for all to see.[11] And this new way of understanding Eucharist become a resounding 'yes' to creation, a living hope that does not disappoint.

Wedding

for Mary and Pat

Where the memory's cloud is thin
we spot the original blue,
harvests brought in, life stirring.

Some local colour, smudge of season
is telling how it always is
in the beginning – the word nursed

into meaning, tree and field
holding hands, every wild flower
in its yes. A homing instinct

draws us in our Sunday best
as one love speaks for all,
joins east and west, lifting
the latch on years and dreams.[12]

Notes

Introduction

1. John Feehan, article 'The Dipper's Acclaim' in *Resurgence*, Satish Kumar, Lorna Howarth, Sophie Poklewiski Koziel (eds), November / December 2003, p 7

2. Joseph Cardinal Ratzinger, *The Spirit of the Liturgy*, San Francisco, Ignatius Press, 2000, p 82

3. Ibid., p 24

4. Ibid., p 34

5. G. K. Chesterton, 'Orthodoxy', quoted in Toolan, David, *At Home in the Cosmos*, Maryknoll, New York, Orbis Books, 2001, p vii

6. Aldo Leopold, *A Sand County Almanac: and Sketches Here and There*, New York, Oxford University Press,1949, pp 203-4

7. Patrick Kavanagh, poem 'Canal Bank Walk' as found in *Lifelines 2: Letters from Famous People about their Favourite Poem*, Dublin, Town House, 1994, p 11

8. Thomas Berry, *The Dream of the Earth*, San Francisco, Sierra Club Books, 1988

9. Thomas Berry, *The Great Work: Our Way into the Future*, New York, Bell Tower, 1999. According to H. Paul Santmire, the attempts by writers from a Christian perspective to deal with the environmental crisis and related cosmic anxieties take up three positions ('schools') though no single writer can easily be so classified. He believes that Thomas Berry along with Matthew Fox and eco-feminists generally are 'deconstructionists' who find the Christian tradition ecologically deficient and so must find new foundations and new categories by which to express their vision. Then there are the 'apologists' whose approach is to defend the tradition for its encouragement of the 'good steward-ship' of the earth and its concern with social justice. This is the position of the World Council of Churches. The 'revisionist' position, within which he places his own explorations, attempts to reclaim, rediscover and retell the Christian story from an ecological perspective. Among advocates, he includes Joseph Sittler, Denis Edwards and Jürgen Moltmann. My own work would

have sympathy with this approach. (*Nature Reborn: the Ecological and Cosmic Promise of Christian Theology*, Minneapolis, Fortress Press, 2000, pp 6-10).

10. Pierre Teilhard de Chardin, 'The Mass on the World' and 'The Spiritual Power of Matter' found in *Hymn of the Universe*, London, Collins, 1965. For Santmire, Teilhard's was a major work of re-visioning but needs to be interpreted within a different context to offset its anthropocentric bias where the material world was granted only instrumental value in furthering the human-Christian project. (*Nature Reborn*, pp 53-60)

11. Pope John Paul II, article, 'God Made Man the Steward of Creation,' *L'Osservatore Romano*, Vatican City, 24 January 2001, p 11

12. Arne Naess, 'Self Realization: An Ecological Approach to Being in the World' in John Seed, Joanna Macy, Pat Fleming, Arne Naess, *Thinking like a Mountain: Towards a Council of all Beings*, Gabriola Island, BC, New Society Publishers, 1988, p 24

13. Leonardo Boff, *Cry of the Earth, Cry of the Poor*, Maryknoll, New York, Orbis, 1997, p 111

14. Rosemary Radford Ruether, ed, *Women Healing Earth: Third World Women on Ecology, Feminism, and Religion*, London, SCM, 1996, p 6

15. Ibid., p 5

16. Pierre Teilhard de Chardin, *Hymn of the Universe*, 'The Mass on the World', London, Collins, 1965, p 24

Chapter 1: A Cosmic Context

1. Joseph Cardinal Ratzinger, *The Spirit of the Liturgy*, p 70

2. Seamus Heaney, 'Mossbawn: Two Poems in Dedication, 1 Sunlight' in *North*, London, Faber and Faber, 1975

3. Seamus Heaney, 'Out of this World' in *District and Circle*, London, Faber and Faber, 2006

4. Damayanthi M. A. Niles, 'A Common Hope Is Always Context-Specific' in Bruggemann, Walter, (ed) *Hope for the World: Mission in a Global Context*, Louisville, Kentucky, Westminster John Knox Press, 2001, p 107-8

5. John Feehan, *Educating for Environmental Awareness*, University College Dublin, Environmental Institute, 1995, p 8

6. Walter Cardinal Kasper, *Sacrament of Unity: The Eucharist and the Church*, New York, A Herder & Herder Book, The Crossroad Publishing Company, 2004, p 127

7. Ibid., p 127

8. John Feehan, article 'The Dipper's Acclaim' in *Resurgence*, Satish Kumar, Lorna Howarth, Sophie Poklewski Koziel (eds), November/December, 2003, pp 7

The dipper *cinclus cinclus* is a dumpy aquatic bird with a short tail which breeds along fast-flowing streams and rivers. Its adaptation to its home place includes being able to swim under-water using its wings (a third white eye-lid protects the eye when submerged), walk along the bottom with the wings held out to prevent it bobbing up, and swim on the surface while making dives into the water. The name 'dipper' refers to its habit of 'curtseying' when perched. Its call is a penetrating 'zits'; its song a slow, soft warbling.

9. Leonardo Boff, *Cry of the Earth, Cry of the Poor*, 1997, p 189

10. Tumani Mutasa Nyajeka, 'Shona Women and the Mutupo Principle,' in *Women Healing Earth*, ed. Rosemary Radford Ruether, London, SCM Press, 1996, p 138

11. John Feehan, quoting from C. Plummer's 'Vitae Sanctorum Hiberniae' in *Farming in Ireland, History, Heritage and Environment*, University College Dublin, Faculty of Agriculture, 2003, p 215

12. James Lovelock, *The Revenge of Gaia: Why the Earth is Fighting Back – and How We Can Still Save Humanity*, London, Allen Lane an imprint of Penguin Books, 2006, p 137

13. Eavan Boland, 'The Emigrant Irish' in *New Collected Poems*, Manchester, Carcanet, 2005, p 158

14. Bao Ruowang, extract, 'Three Scenes from A Labour Camp' in *Captured Voices: An Anthology of Prose and Poems presented by John McCarthy*, edited by Janna Letts and Fiona Whytehead, London, Indigo, an imprint of Orion Books Ltd, 2000, p 116

15. Pierre Teilhard de Chardin, *Hymn of the Universe*, 'The Mass on the World', p 23

16. Denis Edwards, *The God of Evolution, A Trinitarian Theology*, Mahwah, New Jersey, Paulist Press, 1999, (Edwards quoting Richard Dawkins), p 25

17. Willian Blake, 'The Tyger' in *Poems and Letters Selected by Jacob Bronowski*, Middlesex, Penguin Books, 1985

18. Edward P. Echlin, *The Cosmic Circle: Jesus & Ecology*, (reference to John Paul II's encyclical, *Dominus et Vivificantem*. 50.3) Dublin, Columba, 2004, p 150. 'The Incarnation of God the Son

signifies the taking up into unity with God ... the whole of humanity, the entire visible and material world. The Incarnation, then, also has a cosmic significance, a cosmic dimension.'

19. St Anselm, *A Reading from the Discourses of St Anselm*, Or 52, in *The Divine Office: The Liturgy of the Hours according to the Roman Rite*, Vol 1, Dublin, The Talbot Press, 1974, p 25*

20. Collins, Paul, *God's Earth: Religion as if Matter Really Mattered*, Dublin, Gill & Macmillan, 1995, p 241

21. Ibid., p 243

22. Seán Freyne, 'The Quest for the Historical Jesus-Some Theological Reflections,' in *Texts, Contexts and Cultures*, Dublin, Veritas, 2002, p 119

23. Gerard Manley Hopkins, 'God's Grandeur,' in *Poems and Prose of Gerard Manley Hopkins*, Selected and edited by W. H. Gardner, Middlesex, Penguin Books Ltd, 1981, p 24. See 1 Jn 1:1-2: 'something which has existed since the beginning, that we have *heard*, and we have *seen* with our own eyes; that we have *watched* and *touched* with our hands.'

24. Seán McDonagh, *The Death of Life*, Dublin, Columba, 2004, p 94, (referring to Denis Edwards' book, *Breath of Life: A Theology of the Creator Spirit*.)

25. Elizabeth Johnson, A., *Women, Earth and Creator Spirit*, Mahwah, New Jersey, Paulist Press, 1993, p 20

26. Ibid., p 19. The Greek Orthodox theologian, John Zizioulas, is wholly resistant to a christology that ignores the biblical accounts of the role of the Spirit in the life of Christ and that portrays the Spirit as merely 'the janitor who opens the door and lets people into Christ.' (Patricia A. Fox, *God as Communion: John Zizioulas, Elizabeth Johnson and the Retrieval of the Symbol of the Triune God*, Minnesota, A Michael Glazier Book, 2001, p 78). Santmire recalls Irenaeus: 'the Word and the Spirit are "the hands of God"' (*Nature Reborn*, p 56).

27. Seán McDonagh, *The Death of Life*, p 92

28. Seán McDonagh, *The Greening of the Church*, London, Geoffrey Chapman, 1990, p 142

29. Walter Cardinal Kasper, *Sacrament of Unity: The Eucharist and the Church*, New York, Herder & Herder, 2004, p 128

Chapter 2: Telling the New Story

1. Robert Penn Warren, poem, 'Tell me a Story' in *Slow Time: 100 Poems to Take You There*, ed, Niall MacMonagle, Dublin, Marino Books, 2000, p 153

2. Chet Raymo, *Climbing Brandon: Science and Faith on God's Holy Mountain*, Brandon, 2004, p 144

3. John Gribbin, and Simon Goodwin, *Origins: Our Place in Hubble's Universe*, London, Constable, 1997, p 26

4. Jon Turney, *Lovelock & Gaia*, Cambridge, Icon Books, 2003, p 62

5. Ibid., p 67

6. James Lovelock, *The Revenge of Gaia; Why the Earth is Fighting Back – and How We Can Still Save Humanity*, p 25

7. Ibid., p 17

8. Brian Swimme and Thomas Berry, *The Universe Story: From the Primordial Flaring Forth to the Ecozoic Era – A Celebration of the Unfolding of the Cosmos*, New York, Harper San Francisco, 1994, p 51

9. Seán McDonagh, *Climate Change: the Challenge to all of us*, Dublin, Columba, 2006, (quotation from Pope Benedict XVI, Fides Services, 7 November 2005), p 174

10. Swimme and Berry, *The Universe Story*, p 249

11. Ibid., p 45

12. Ibid., p 250

13. Ibid., pp. 73-7

14. Pierre Teilhard de Chardin, 'The Mass on the World' in *Hymn of the Universe*, p 32

15. Brian Swimme, *The Universe is a Green Dragon: A Cosmic Creation Story*, Rochester, Vemont, Bear & Company, 2001, p 40

16. Joseph Cardinal Ratzinger, *The Spirit of the Liturgy*, p 68

17. Ibid., p 108

18. Pope Benedict XVI, *The Consecrated Host Truly is the Bread of Heaven*, homily on the Feast of Corpus Christi at the Basilica of St John Lateran, Rome, 15 June 2006

19. Alan Lightman, 'How the Camel Got his Hump' in *Dance for Two*, selected essays, London, Bloomsbury 1996, p 144

20. Rachel Carson, *Silent Spring*, America: Houghton Mifflin, 1962, reprinted London, Penguin Classics, 2000, pps 21-2

21. Ibid., p 75

22. Ibid., p 239

23. Ibid., p 264

24. Ibid., p 169

25. (Jiddu) Krishnamurti, *Krishnamurti's Notebook*, New York, HarperSanFrancisco, 1984, p 208

26. *General Instruction of the Roman Missal*, Irish Catholic Bishops' Conference, Dublin, Irish Liturgical Publications, 2005, par 15

27. John McGahern, *That They May Face the Rising Sun*, London, Faber and Faber, 2002, p 25

28. J. (Jiddu) Krishnamurti, *Beginnings of Learning*, Phoenix 2003, p 27

29. John Feehan, *Background to a Poem for Hui-Tsung, Poems 1968-73*, Cape Town, Salesian Press, 1974

Chapter 3: The Implications of an Ecological Conversion for our Celebration of the Eucharist

1. Patrick Kavanagh, 'The Great Hunger' in *Collected Poems*, London, Martin Brian and O'Keefe, 1972, p 38

2. Pope John Paul II, 'God made man the steward of creation', *L'Osservatore Romano*, Vatican City, 24 January 2001, p 11

3. Seán McDonagh, *Climate Change: The challenge to all of us*, Dublin, Columba, 2006, p 163-4

4. Joseph Cardinal Ratzinger, *The Spirit of the Liturgy*, p 82. Such an important perspective can be identified in Pope Benedict's Post Synodal Exhortation on the Eucharist, *Sacramentum Caritatis*, London, CTS, 2007, (pars 12, 16, 30, 31, 47, 92). Nevertheless, it does seem like an opportunity missed to draw a closer relationship between the celebration of the Eucharist and the multiple threats to life on the earth. This statement from the salient paragraph 92, 'The Sanctification of the World and the Protection of Creation' is barely adequate: 'The justified concern about threats to the environment present in so many parts of the world is reinforced by Christian hope, which commits us to working responsibly for the protection of creation.' And though the relationship is addressed – 'the Eucharist powerfully illuminates human history and the whole cosmos' – the embedded nature of our existence within creation is unacknowledged. It's as if climate change, for instance, (not mentioned here), were not an essential part of our response in faith and worship. In H. Paul Santmire's schema (Introduction, note 9), the ecological perspective of this Exhortation belongs to the 'apologist' school.

5. Edward O. Wilson, *The Future of Life*, London, A Little Brown Book, 2002, p 151

6. Patrick Kavanagh, 'If Ever You Go To Dublin Town' in *No Earthly Estate: God and Patrick Kavanagh: an Anthology*, selected by Tom Stack, Dublin, Columba, 2002

7. e. e. cummings, 'pity this busy monster, manunkind' in *100 Selected Poems*, New York, Grove Press, 1959

8. *Gaudium et Spes*, Pastoral Constitution on the Church in the Modern World, *The Documents of Vatican II*, London-Dublin, Geoffrey Chapman, 1966

9. *Catechism of the Catholic Church*, Dublin, Veritas, 1995

10. Joseph Cardinal Ratzinger, *The Spirit of the Liturgy*, p 97

11. James Lovelock, 'Making Peace with Gaia' in *Resurgence*, p 61

12. Stan Rowe, article, 'Earth Alive' in *Resurgence*, March/April 2003, p 58

13. Pope John Paul II, *Sollicitudo Rei Socialis* (On Social Concern), Washington DC, USCC, January 1988, par 34

14. Seán McDonagh, *Why are we Deaf to the Cry of the Poor?* Dublin, Veritas, 2001, p 41

15. Pope John Paul II, *Letter to Artists*, Chicago, Liturgy Training Publications, 1999, par 1

16. Gerard Manley Hopkins, 'God's Grandeur,' in *Poems and Prose of Gerard Manley Hopkins*, Middlesex, Penguin Books, 1981, p 27

17. E. F. Schumacher, *This I Believe*, A Resurgence Book, an imprint of Green Books Ltd, 1998, p 30

18. Pierre Teilhard de Chardin, *Hymn of the Universe*, 'The Spiritual Power of Matter', pp 61-2

19. Rachel Carson, *Silent Spring*, 'Afterword' by Linda Lear, pp 261-2

20. Vincent MacNamara, *New Life For Old: On Desire and Human Becoming*, Dublin, Columba 2004, pp 81-2

21. Dylan Thomas, 'The Hand that Signed the Paper,' in *Collected Poems 1934-1952*, London, Dent, 1978

22. Pandurang Hegde, 'Silent Revolution' in *New Internationalist*, October 2005, p 16

23. *The Year of the Eucharist: Suggestions and Proposals*, Congregation for Divine Worship and the Discipline of the Sacraments, Dublin, Veritas, 2005, par 28

24. Maura 'Soshin' O'Halloran, *Pure Heart, Enlightened Mind*, London, Thorsons, an imprint of HarperCollins Publishers, 1994, p 109

25. Eckhart Tolle, *Stillness Speaks: Whispers of Now*, London, Hodder and Stoughton, A Mobius Book, 2003, p 78

26. Eckhart Tolle, *The Power of Now: A Guide to Spiritual Enlightenment*, London, Hodder and Stoughton, 2001, p 79

27. Ibid., p 65

28. Archbishop Dermot Clifford, *The Whole of Creation is Groaning*, Pastoral Letter on the Environment, Catholic Communications Office, Dublin, 10/3/2003

29. Dag Hammarskjold, *Markings*, London, Faber and Faber, 1975, p 148

30. Thomas Berry, *The Great Work*, p 67

31. David Toolan, *At Home in the Cosmos*, New York, Orbis Books, 2001, p 243

32. Edward O. Wilson, *The Future of Life*, p 16

Chapter 4: Celebrating Eucharist in a Holy Communion

1. Peter Sirr, 'China,' in *Selected Poems: 1982-2004*, Oldcastle, Co Meath, Ireland, Gallery Press, 2004, pp 70-71

2. Seamus Heaney, 'The Given Note' in *Door into the Dark*, London, Faber, 1969, p 46

3. George Herbert, 'The Church Porch' in *Poet to Poet, George Herbert selected by W. H. Auden*, Middlesex, England, Penguin Books, 1973, p 15

4. John Paul II, *God Made Man the Steward of Creation*, General Audience, 17 January 2001, www.vatican.va

5. Aldo Leopold, *A Sand County Almanac: and Sketches Here and There*, p viii

6. Pope Benedict XVI, *The Consecrated Host Truly Is the Bread of Heaven*, sermon on the Feast of Corpus Christi at the Basilica of St John Lateran on 15 June 2006, Vatican Information Service

7. Patricia A. Fox, *God as Communion; John Zizioulas, Elizabeth Johnson, and the Retrieval of the Symbol of the Triune God*, Minnesota, A Michael Glazier Book, published by the Liturgical Press, Collegeville, Minnesota, 2001, p 59

8. Ibid., p 66. For a succinct account of Zizioulas' reflections on Eucharist and ecological conversion see Denis Edwards, *Ecology*

at the Heart of Faith, Orbis Books, New York, 2006, pp 99-102

9. 'Lumen Gentium, Dogmatic Constitution on the Church', *The Documents of Vatican II*, London-Dublin, Geoffrey Chapman, 1966, par 36. See also pars 32, 33 and especially 34; 'as worshippers, whose every deed is holy, the laity consecrate the world to God.'

10. Seán McDonagh, *The Death of Life*, story attributed to Belden C. Lane, Dublin, Columba Press, p 109-110

11. Pope Benedict XVI, *The Consecrated Host Truly Is the Bread of Heaven*

12. Ibid.

13. John Lane, *Timeless Beauty: in the Arts and Everyday Life*, Devon, Green Books, 2003, pp 162-3, (prayer: version taken from inside page)

Conclusion

1. A Consensus Paper, 'Hope from Old Sources for a New Century', in Walter Bruggemann, (ed), *Hope for the World: Mission in a Global Context*, Louisville, Kentucky, WJK, 2001, p 16

2. Derek Walcott, 'Bright Opposite of Nothing,' in *Poetry Ireland Review*, issue 43/44, Chris Agee (ed), Special North American Issue, Autumn/Winter 1994, p 1

3. 1996 UN Food Summit – Hope for the Hungry? found at www.columban.ie

4. Leonardo Boff, *Ecology & Liberation: A New Paradigm*, Maryknoll, New York, Orbis Books, 2002 (5th printing), p 161

5. Pierre Teilhard de Chardin, 'The Mass on the World', p 22

6. E. F. Schumacher, *This I Believe*, p 211. 'The cardinal virture of prudence presupposes an orientation of the whole person towards the ultimate goal of life … If nature is currently telling us in her own language that we are threatening her health and life-sustaining power, we have obviously been failing in the virtue of prudence and have not been able to see things as they really are.'

7. John Lane, *Timeless Beauty: In the Arts and Everday Life*, pp 92-4

8. Walter Cardinal Kasper, *Sacrament of Unity: The Eucharist and the Church*, pp 141-2

9. Brian Swimme, *The Universe is a Green Dragon*, p 18

10. Patricia A. Fox, *God as Communion: John Zizioulas, Elizabeth Johnson and the Retrieval of the Symbol of the Triune God*, p 231.

11. The Greek word, *aggareuein*, translated as 'requisition', 'force' or 'compel' is a technical term from the Roman military vocabulary. It is used only twice in the New Testament, appearing in Mt 5:41 and Mt 27:32. Joseph Ratzinger interprets this latter use of the term (regarding Simon of Cyrene), as 'letting oneself be taken into service by the loving and suffering Christ ... for the least of the brethren in whom he is suffering, so as with him to bear the yoke of his "yes".' (*The Yes of Jesus Christ*, p 108)

12. Hugh O'Donnell, 'Wedding' in *Scraps for the Feast*, Salesian Press, Pallaskenry, Co Limerick, 1993, p 41. For a theological articulation of 'the nuptial character of the Eucharist' see Pope Benedict's Exhortation, *Sacramentum Caritatis* 2007, par 27